Form and Meaning in Mahesh Dattani's Plays

Form and Meaning in Mahesh Dattani's Plays

Bijay Kumar Das

ATLANTIC
PUBLISHERS & DISTRIBUTORS (P) LTD

Published by

ATLANTIC

PUBLISHERS & DISTRIBUTORS (P) LTD

7/22, Ansari Road, Darya Ganj,
New Delhi-110002
Phones : +91-11-40775252, 23273880, 23275880, 23280451
Fax : +91-11-23285873
Web : www.atlanticbooks.com
E-mail : orders@atlanticbooks.com

Branch Office
5, Nallathambi Street, Wallajah Road,
Chennai-600002
Phones : +91-44-64611085, 32413319
E-mail : chennai@atlanticbooks.com

Printed in India at Glorious Printers, A-13, D.S.I.D.C., Jhilmil Industrial Area, Delhi-110095

Dedicated to

My son, Soumen

and

Daughter, Sonali

Who ask for more

ACKNOWLEDGEMENTS

Acknowledgements are due to *The Critical Endeavour* and *The Journal of Indian Writing in English* in which two of the chapters were published in December 2007 and January 2008 respectively. Special thanks are due to Mahesh Dattani who answered my queries by e-mail.

Bijay Kumar Das

Preface

Mahesh Dattani needs no introduction. He shot into fame with the winning of Sahitya Akademi Award for *Final Solutions and Other Plays* in 1998. Two volumes of his plays entitled *Collected Plays* bear Penguin India imprint.

A theatre personality, Dattani is actively involved in stage production and performing on stage, drawing inspiration from the Marathi playwright Vijay Tendulkar. But unlike Girish Karnad—who lays emphasis on history, myths and scriptures—Dattani concentrates on contemporary society and reality in the fast changing world. His plays are topical dramas, and the questions he addresses are those relating to feminine identity, religion, communal tension and sexuality. What one loves in his plays is the fascinating way in which he presents the dynamics of personal and moral choices while focusing on human relationships.

Modern Indian Theatre came into being with the establishment of Sangeet Natak Akademi, the National Academy of Music and Dance Drama and the National School of Drama in the 1950s and '60s. The best known four playwrights—Mohan Rakesh, Girish Karnad, Badal Sircar and Vijay Tendulkar—dominated the Indian Theatre for quite a long time. Mahesh Dattani appeared on the horizon in the 1980s and revolutionised both Indian English play and theatre.

Dattani is a multi-faceted personality. Apart from being a prolific playwright, he is an actor and director par excellence.

He has attracted lots of attention from the media and theatre personalities. What distinguishes him from other playwrights is his courage of conviction in depicting innovative themes like portrayal of sex preferences by men and women which were until recently considered to be taboos in our society. He seems to say that our fate lies not in the stars but in our own hands.

This book is written with the purpose of evaluating his plays for the benefit of students, researchers and teachers who want to study them critically for academic purpose. I shall be glad if this book finds favour with them.

I would like to thank Atlantic Publishers and Distributors (P) Ltd., for bringing out this book.

Bijay Kumar Das

Contents

Introduction

1

At the outset, I would like to state clearly about the distination between Modern Indian Theatre and Modern Indian English plays. Modern Indian Theatre came into being with the establishment of Sangeet Natak Akademi, the National Music and Drama Academy and the National School of Drama in the nineteen fifties and sixties. Mostly plays written in Hindi and translated into Hindi dominated the Indian Theatre. Just like the big trio (Mulk Raj Anand, R.K. Narayan and Raja Rao) in Indian English fiction, the best known four—Mohan Rakesh (Hindi), Girish Karnad (Kannada), Badal Sircar (Bengali) and Vijay Tendulkar (Marathi) dominated the Indian Theatre for a pretty long time. And then came Mahesh Dattani, who revolutionised both Indian English plays and Theatre. As Paul wrote in *Indian International Centre Quarterly*:

> To the language writers, a Hindi production of their play was the thing. Every important playwright—be it Girish Karnad in Kannada, Badal Sircar in Bengali or Vijay Tendulkar in Marathi—sought the company of Hindi theatre directors, both in their respective regions and in Delhi. Three or four translators served as the important links: B.V. Karnath for Kannada, Pratibha Agrawal and Santwana for Bengali, and Vasant Dev for Marathi. Hindi theatre groups in regional language-dominated areas thus became good sounding boards. They operated in a small, unostentatious manner to present unestablished contemporary plays, while Hindi theatre groups in Delhi like Dishantar, Abhiyan and the

> National School of Drama helped in inter-regional translation of these plays: Kannada plays into Bengali and Bengali plays into Marathi. Sometimes the availability of these plays in English translation accelerated the process of cross-fertilization. Thus, when in 1969 *Enact* started publishing the full length plays of these important playwrights in English translations, it helped satisfy the appetite of most new converts to theatre who could not read the script in the original or in its Hindi version. English formed the necessary link. (8)

It is a fact that regional playwrights started translating their plays or getting their plays translated into English and Hindi after independence. "Though both English and Hindi continue to share the honour of being the two most important target languages of translation. English being the more important when it comes to print, making as it does for national visibility—Hindi outspaces English when it comes to performance and the issue of audience appeal" (Dalmia, 7).

However, the original playwriting in English continues unabated despite the lack of scope for production in Theatre. It's a fact that in the last one hundred and seventy-seven years (i.e. between 1831 and 2007), we have hundreds of plays written in English in our country. Of these hardly fifteen to twenty dramatists have made their mark in that genre.

For a diachronic study of Indian English drama mention may be made of Krishna Mohan Banerjee who wrote the first ever Indian English play, *The Persecuted or Dramatics Scenes Illustrative of the Present State of Hindu Society in Calcutta* in 1831. Forty years after Michael Madhusudan Dutt published his, *Is This Called Civilization?* (1871). This is an English rendering of his Bengali play. We take it as an Indian English play in the same way we take Girish Karnad's plays as Indian English Plays, for he has transcreated them into English. As K.R.S. Iyengar has rightly observed: "Sri Aurobindo's *Perseus the Deliverer, Vasavdutta, Rodogune, The Vizers of Bassore* and *Eric*...were written in English as original dramatic creations.... All five plays underline the need for Love, for Love alone is the great solvent of all varieties of evil. Love is supreme truth and goodness and power and it can defy death and conquer it, and turn dross into gold" (226-31).

The next important playwright is Harindranath Chattopadhyaya. His *Five Plays* (1937) is marked by realism and social consciousness. Other important Indian English playwrights are T.P. Kailasam [*The Burden and Fulfilment* (1933), *The Purpose* (1944) and *Karna: the Brahmin's Curse* (1946)], Bharati Sarabhai [*The Well of the People* (1943), *Two Women* (1952)], A.S.P. Ayyar [*In the Clutch of the Devil* (1926), *Sita's Choice and Other Plays* (1935), *The Slave of Ideas and Other Plays* (1941), *The Trial of Science for the Murder of Humanity* (1942)], G.V. Desani (*Hati* 1950), Asif Currimbhoy [*The Doldrummers* (1960), *The Dumb Dancer* (1961), *Goa* (1964)], Pratap Sharma [*A Touch of Brightness* (1968)], Gieve Patel (*Princess*, 1970), Gurcharan Das (*Larins Sahib,* 1970), T.S. Gill (*Asoka*, 1983), Dina Mehta [*The Myth Makers* (1969), *Brides Area Not for Burning* (1993)] and Manjula Padmanabhan (*Harvest,* 1998). Three plays, *Lights Out* by Manjula Padmanabhan, *Getting Away with Murder* by Dina Mehta and *Mangalam* by Poile Sengupta have appeared in *Body Blows: Women, Violence and Survival: Three Plays* (2000). Having mentioned the names of some well known and some not so well known playwrights in Indian English Literature, it may be mentioned here that in spite of plays being written in English in our country, these plays have not taken roots in our soil due to the lack of production and performance.

Notwithstanding a number of plays written earlier, Indian English drama has no tradition to fall back on. However, we have a few Indian English playwrights who have tried their hands at playwriting and achieved limited success. In this connection the names of only two playwrights, i.e. Asif Currimbhoy and Nissim Ezekiel come to our mind, who achieved, success to some extent. Currimbhoy's *Goa* and Ezekiel's *Three Plays* and *Don't Call It Suicide* can be taken as a source of inspiration for other playwrights to pursue writing plays in English. Girish Karnad, a Theatre and film personality is a successful playwright. But most of his plays are originally written in Kannada and then transcreated into English. Moreover, he like Rabindranath Tagore turns to Indian epics and myths for his themes. Mahesh Dattani, a theatre personality who is actually involved in stage production and performing on the stage, draws inspiration from Marathi playwright, Vijay Tendulkar. Unlike Girish Karnad who lays emphasis on history, myths and purans, Dattani concentrates on contemporary society and reality in the fast changing world. He is a playwright on contemporary urban India and his plays are topical dramas. The questions he addresses in his plays are those of gender, sex, religion, communal tension, feminine identity, same-sex marriage, and above all, gay and lesbian relationship. Hence, his plays appear to be revolting, sometimes, outrageous.

Dramatic criticism centers round the meaning of the plays, first and techniques, afterwards. Like, Harold Pinter, the Nobel Prize Winner for Literature for 2006, Dattani believes in the production of his plays. The play is the meaning—it means what it says. Dattani's two collections of his plays titled, *Collected Plays* (2000) and *Collected Plays* Vol. II (2005) have appeared in Penguin India imprint. Most of his plays were staged in Bangalore and Mumbai. Some of them were broadcast on Radio and B.B.C. The first collection contains eight plays such as *Seven Steps Around the Fire*, *On a Muggy Night in Mumbai*, *Do the Needful*, *Final Solutions*, *Bravely Fought the Queen*, *Tara*, *Dance Like a Man* and *Where There's a Will*. And the second collection contains ten plays—eight new and two of his early plays, *Dance Like a Man* and *Seven Steps Around the Fire*. The eight new plays are *Thirty Days in September*, *Clearing the Rubble*, *Mango Souffle*, *The Swami and Winston*, *Morning Raga*, *Uma and the Fairy Queen*, *Ek Alag Mausam* and *The Tale of a Mother Feeding Her Child*. The total corpus of his plays which include Radio plays, Screen plays and Stage plays is sixteen. He came to limelight and shot into fame with the winning of the first ever Sahitya Akademi Award for a playwright in 1998 for his work *Final Solutions* and *Other Plays*.

In this opening chapter, an attempt has been made to lay emphasis on the making of the playwright. Dattani was involved in the Theatre during his school and college days. And later on, he acted in plays and then directed plays and started his Theatre company. At the initial stage of his involvement in the translation and direction of plays, he had not planned to become a playwright. It was under the influence of Vijay Tendulkar and later on, Tennessee Williams, he began writing plays. He makes this clear in course of an interview with Sachidananda Mohanty in the following passage:

> Well, I was particularly impressed by the plays of Vijay Tendulkar. Actually, that was one of the reasons why I decided to write myself, because when I saw plays in Hindi or Gujarati and I managed to acquire the translation, they just didn't have the same impact. *Silence, the Court is in Session!* was such a brilliant play, but I felt that the translation in English threw away most of the effect. Later on, it was Tennessee Williams. I relate to Tennessee Williams because he writes about vulnerable women in a very violent society. I think I tend to do that as well, although I don't see my woman as vulnerable, in the sense that they do fight their battles. They are not on the winning side of the battle, and I think I have learnt a lot about dramatic structure. (*CP* 13:2 173)

Though Dattani was impressed by Marathi theatre and less enthusiastic about Gujarati theatre, he chose to write his plays in English. He makes his stand clear on the question of the language in which he writes in an interview given to Ranu Uniyal in the following passage:

> My mother tongue is Gujarati. My Mom doesn't know English and even with my Dad I conversed in Gujarati (my father passed away in 2000) and it's only amongst the siblings, my two sisters and I, that we speak in English because all three of us received an education where the first language, that is, the medium of instruction was English, and of course, we were encouraged to speak in English at a very young age because that was seen as the language of the future...writing plays really happened more out of necessity because I wanted to do more Indian plays in English. But the translations that were available didn't do justice to the original. So I thought why not try my hand in writing the plays myself and it's quite ironic that what I began to do out of necessity became a

> passion. Later I had my theatre company in Bangalore and at the moment a studio theatre just two streets from where I live devoted entirely to new writing in English. And I do workshops for playwrights and actors and directors as well and I see it as a laboratory for new works, interesting new works. (*CP* 13:2 176-77)

Well known theatre personalities, such as directors, producers and actors have written introduction to Dattani's plays included in the two volumes published by Penguin Books in 2000 and 2005. These include the names of Lillette Dubey, Jeremy Mortimer, Mithran Devanesen, Sanjeev Shah, Shabana Azmi, Sally Avens, John McRae, Erin Mee, Sita Raina, Alyque Padamsee and Michael Walling. Let us take some of the significant statements made by these important personalities on the dramatic art of Dattani:

> As I suggested in the introduction to *Final Solutions and Other Plays* (1994), his special theatrical quality to build tension in a social context, leading to a classic dramatic confrontation which involves not only the characters themselves, but which also confronts the audiences with its expectations and attitudes. (John McRae, 'A Note on the Play', *Collected Plays* 46)

Mahesh's plays often feature characters who are questioning their identity, and who feel isolated in some way. (Jeremy Mortimer, 'A Note on the Play', *Collected Plays*, 4).

> "His plays fuse the physical and special awareness of the Indian theatre with the textual rigour of western models like Ibsen and Tennessee Williams. It's a potent combination, which shocks and disturbs through its accuracy and its ability to approach a subject from multiple perspectives. Postcolonial India and multi-cultural Britain both have an urgent need for a cultural expression of the contemporary, they require public spaces in which the mingling of eastern and western influences can take place. Through his fusion of forms and influences Mahesh creates such a space. This is in itself a political and social statement of astonishing force". (Michael Walling 'A Note on the Play,' *Collected Plays* 229).

Mahesh Dattani frequently takes as his subject the complicated dynamics of the modern urban family. His characters struggle for some kind of freedom and happiness under the weight of tradition, cultural constructions of gender, and repressed desire. Their dramas are played out on multi-level sets where interior and exterior become one, and geographical locations are collapsed—in short, his settings are as fragmented as the families who inhabit them. In his plays, Dattani takes on what he called the 'invisible issues' of Indian society. (Erin Mee, 'Note on the Play,' *Collected Plays* 320)

It will be helpful if we take Dattani's own views on his plays and how he became a playwright, along with the comments by critics stated above. That will be a correct perspective to understand, analyse and appreciate his plays. In course of an interview Datani states:

'You can talk about feminism, because in a way that is accepted. But you can't talk about gay issues because that's not Indian, [that] doesn't happen here. You can't talk about a middle-class housewife fantasizing about having sex with the cook or actually having a sex life—that isn't Indian either—that's confrontational even if it is Indian.' By pulling taboo subjects out from under the rug and placing them on stage for public discussion, Dattani challenges the constructions of 'India' and 'Indian' as they have traditionally been defined in modern theatre. He encourages other playwrights to do the same: 'Our culture is so rich with tradition, and that's a great advantage and a great disadvantage as well, because...we're living in the present and there are so many challenges facing us—you just have to cross the road and you have an issue,...I think it is very important for our country to spawn new playwrights...who reflect honestly and purely our lives, because...that is our contribution to the world.' (qtd. in Erin Mee 319)

Speaking of the need for poetic licence in a play, Dattani underlines the following:

Should the play be read in classrooms, I sincerely wish that English language teachers and staunch Wren and Martinites

> will not dismiss my syntax as bad English, or worse still, as incorrect. While knowledge of the rules of grammar is important, the richness and variety of the spoken word is a study in itself. (qtd. in Ramaswamy 278-79)

Mahesh Dattani acknowledges his indebtedness to two directors, Alyque Padamsee and Lillete Dubey who helped him to build his self-esteem and confidence by their production of his plays. Alyque's comments, "At last a playwright with some conviction" encouraged Dattani to write more plays. Dattani says, "Alyque believed in my work even before I believed in it myself. He gave me the courage to call myself a professional playwright and director" (Preface to *Collected Plays* XII). And about Lillette, Dattani says,

> Many years later, after Alyque had produced successful productions of *Tara* and *Final Solutions,* Lillette chose to do *Dance Like a Man.* At that point I don't think anyone knew that the play will create some sort of a record doing more than a hundred shows in India, London, Dubai and Colombo, and God knows where else Lillette wants to take it. Unheard of for a silly Indian play in English about retired Bharatanatyam dancers to meet with such success. I think a large part of its success goes to Lillette's vividly limned portrayal of Ratna, a woman confronting the demons created by her past and present actions.... Lillete pulled off the impossible task of making a commercial success of *On a Muggy Night in Mumbai,* a play about the travails of gay men and women, some of them strongly anti-heterosexual. Never in any wildest imagination did I expect this play to play to mainstage audiences. It did, thanks to Lillette's perseverance and true grit. (Preface to *Collected Plays* XIV)

From the observations of the directors and theatre personalities and from Dattani's acknowledgements, certain important points about him and his plays emerge.

The most important aspect of Dattani's plays is that they address the "invisible issues" of contemporary Indian society. For instance, the branching out of feminism into same-sex love relationship like homosexuality and lesbianism which are unacceptable to Indian society even today, find a place in Dattani's plays. Gender relationship, and the plight of hijras (eunuchs), who are neither male nor female, but wanting to be both, are artistically as well as realistically presented in his plays.

The second important aspect of Dattani's plays is that they dive deep into human heart and create characters true to life-situations. To watch his plays being enacted on the stage is to see the characters inside out. These characters seek an identity for themselves which is both lovable and enduring. Engrossed in contemporary reality, his characters seek a remedy of their ills and sufferings caused by poverty and societal discrimination.

The third important characteristic of his plays is the family bond that binds its members together or the breaking of that bond through mutual distrust and suspicion. Extra-marital relationship is a favourite subject with Dattani as it is with Girish Karnad. Religious fundamentalism, communal tension, natural calamity like drought which makes people homeless, are some of Dattani's favourite themes.

As a performing artist, Dattani believes in the magic of words. His plays are not meant to be read in the drawing room but to be staged for the audience. Hence, Dattani lays emphasis on stage directions. There are a lot of stage directions in course of play. These elaborate instructions sometimes make the reading of his plays clumsy. Political subjects, crimes of the society and the failure of law and order are some of the other themes of his plays. Social activists, detectives play a major role in some of his plays. If Girish Karnad deals with myths and history, Mahesh Dattani highlights contemporary reality in his plays. It should be noted here that quite a few of his plays are commissioned by B.B.C. His radio and screenplays are very powerful in evoking the empathy of the viewers. Shabana Azmi makes an important observation on Dattani's screen play when she says, "Mahesh's screenplay makes emotional transitions between the lines rather than through the dialogue" (333). She further explains the nature of a screenplay by referring to the observations of Frank Pearson in the following lines:

> According to Frank Pearson, a screenplay means different things to different people. The producer 'weighs' it for

'audience appeal', the director visualizes it as a 'progression of images and scenes', the designer tries to fit into locations and sets, the actor is intent to learn his lines and the assistant director sees it as a schedule. (*CP*, II, 333)

Dattani's plays embody appropriate visual images and the scenes are well designed. He combines in him the skill of a director, the performing art of an actor and above all, the insight of a playwright who 'sees life steadily and sees it whole'. His plays make the readers see into the world of contemporary reality and they recall the characters drawn from the contemporary society, only the real names are changed. Reality and objectivity are the hallmark of Dattani's plays.

WORKS CITED

Azmi, Shabana. "A Note on the Play", *Morning Raga, Collected Plays,* Vol. II, New Delhi: Penguin Books, 2005.

Dalmia, Vasudha. *Poetics, Plays and Performances: The Politics of Modern Indian Theatre.* New Delhi: OUP, 2006.

Dattani, Mahesh. Preface. *Collected Plays.* New Delhi: Penguin Books, 2000.

———. Conversing with Ranu Uniyal. *The Commonwealth Review*, 13: 2, 2002.

———. Interview with Sachidananda Mohanty. *The Commonwealth Review*, 13: 2, 2001.

Iyengar, K.R.S. *Indian Writing in English.* New Delhi: Sterling Publishers, 1984.

McRae, John. "A Note on the Play." *On a Muggy Night in Mumbai. Collected Plays.* New Delhi: Penguin Books, 2000.

Mee, Erin. Quoted. "A Note on the Play". *Tara. Collected Plays.* New Delhi: Penguin Books, 2000.

Mortimer, Jeremy. "A Note on the Play," *Seven Steps Around the Fire, Collected Plays.* New Delhi: Penguin Books, 2000.

Paul, Rajinder. "Whatever Happened to Modern Indian Theatre", *India International Centre Quarterly.* Spring, 1991.

Ramaswamy, S. "Indian Drama in English: A Tentative Reflection". *Makers of Indian English Literature.* Ed. C.D. Narasimhaiah. Delhi: Pencraft International, 2000.

Walling, Michael. "A Note on the Play." *Bravely Fought the Queen. Collected Plays.* New Delhi: Penguin Books, 2000.

2 Themes in Mahesh Dattani's Plays

Modern playwrights avoid questions on the themes of their plays because they feel uncomfortable to answer them. T.S. Eliot, Samuel Beckett, Harold Pinter, to name a few well known playwrights, expressed their displeasure about such questions. Mahesh Dattani too belongs to that group who avoids direct answers to thematic questions on his plays. For these playwrights the play is the thing. But for a reader or critic, themes count much. It is through the themes that they evaluate a playwright and classify his plays. Having said so, let me turn to the themes of Dattani's plays.

While going through the plays of Dattani, one faces a dilemma. That is, how should one approach them: chronologically as they appear in the contents of his two volumes of plays or on the basis of similarity of themes. For example, *Seven Steps Around the Fire, The Swami and Winston* and *Uma and the Fairy Queen* form a triology in which the same researcher, Uma and her husband, Suresh appear. Speaking methodically, the second approach is preferable to the first.

Let us, take those plays first, which are based on crime and unusual love relationship. We should begin with *Seven Steps Around the Fire*. The storyline of this play is unusual in the Indian context. As Jeremy Mortimer puts it:

> For the story he chooses to tell is no ordinary story. The murder victim Kamla, a beautiful hijra (eunuch), had, it turns out, been secretly married to Subbu, the son of a wealthy government minister. The minister had the young

> hijra burned to death, and hastily arranged for his son to marry an acceptable girl. But at the wedding—attended of course by the hijras who sing and dance at weddings and births—Subbu produces a gun and kills himself. The truth behind the suicide is hushed up, but Uma has been keeping full notes for her thesis on the hijras community. (*CP* 3)

As the note to the play states, *Seven Steps Around the Fire* was first broadcast as *Seven Circles Around the Fire* by BBC Radio 4 on 9 January 1999. The play begins with Uma, a Ph.D. scholar in Sociology and wife of the Superintendent of Police, Suresh Rao trying to know from Munswamy, a constable in the office of the Superintendent of Police about the hijra, Anarkali (who is contemptuously referred to 'she' and 'it'). Uma's husband Suresh Rao does not trust the hijras and calls them liars and looks down upon them. Dattani takes care to explain the term 'hijra' by digging up the Indian myth from *The Ramayana* through the mouth of Uma:

> A brief note on the popular myths on the origin of the hijras will be in order, before looking at the class-gender-based power implications. The term hijra, of course, is of Urdu origin, a combination of Hindi, Persian and Arabic, literary meaning 'neither male nor female'. Another legend traces their ancestry to *The Ramayan*. The legend has it that god Rama was going to cross the river and go into exile in the forest. All the people of the city wanted to follow him. He said, 'Men and women, turn back'. Some of his male followers did not know what to do. They could not disobey him. So they sacrificed their masculinity, to become neither men nor women, and followed him to the forest. Rama was pleased with their devotion and blessed them. There are trans-sexuals all over the world, and India is no exception. The purpose of this case study is to show their position in society.
>
> Perceived as the lowest of the low, they yearn for family and love. The two events in mainstream Hindu culture where their presence is acceptable—marriage and birth—ironically are the very same privileges denied to them by man and nature. (10-11)

After verifying the identity of Uma as a teacher of Sociology at Bangalore University and the wife of Suresh Rao, the Superintendent of Police, Anarkali goes on to answer Uma's queries. She says, "What is there to tell? I sing with other hijras at weddings and when a child is born. People give us money, otherwise, I will put a curse on them". Anarkali knows the truth behind Kamla's murder but is afraid to tell it to Uma. She says, "They will kill me also if I tell the truth. If I don't tell the truth, I will die in jail". On the other hand, she asks Uma to go to Russel Market in Shivajinagar and see the hijra Champa and give her money to know the truth.

Uma decides to see Champa and begins to think about the nature of hijra community. Uma (thought):

> Nobody seems to know anything about them. Neither do they. Did they come to this country with Islam, or are they a part of our glorious Hindu tradition? Why are they so obsessed with weddings and ceremonies of childbirth? How do they come to know of these weddings? Why do they just show up without being invited? Are they just extortionists? And why do they not take singing lessons? (Pause.) Is it true? Could it be true what my mother used to say about them? Did they really put a curse on her because they did not allow them to sing and dance at their wedding? Or was that their explanation for not being able to have children of their own? Or...a reason to give to people for wanting to adopt me? (*CP* 16-17)

Uma asked her Vice Chancellor father to give her Rs. 50,000 which she would spend to know the minds of the hijras. Uma told Munswamy, the constable that they were going to see Champa, Anarkali's friend. In spite of the constable's warning, Uma went to Russel Market to see the hijra community. She met Champa and persuaded her to tell the truth about Kamla's murder. Champa gave the key of Kamala's trunk to her and stated clearly that neither she nor Anarkali was a killer. The conversation between her and Uma reveals everything about the hijra community. It is a fact that the head hijra keeps other hijras and uses them for earning a lot. It also becomes clear that Kamla was married to a youngman (the photograph had been taken) and she was murdered. Uma becomes curious to know who was the powerful person who had done such a crime and went scot-free. Uma tells her Professor why she wants to complete the study on the life and occupation of the hijras:

> Professor, this is Uma Rao! Do you have sometime to discuss my paper? ...Well, I will be brief. I am wondering whether I could leave out the case study on the hijras.... Well, it all seems a little too sordid and I find it more and more difficult to do thorough research.... I know there is very little written about them, and now I understand why.... But there is no way I can win their trust! May be there is, but I don't know.... How important is it?... Oh...I guess I will have to.... If my family throws me out, I hope that doctorate will come in handy. (28-29)

Uma is serious about getting at the truth of Kamla's murder. After going home and meeting her husband Suresh, she comes back to Champa and Anarkali. The hijras feel that nobody cares for them in the society and they are treated as unwanted. The following conversation between Anarkali and Uma reveals the agony of being a hijra.

> Anarkali. Then what will you do knowing who killed Kamla?
>
> Uma. Tell my husband to make an arrest.
>
> Anarkali. One hijra less in this world does not matter to your husband. (35)

Since Champa and Anarkali know who killed Kamla and how powerful is he, Anarkali tells Uma, "Don't put your own position in danger. Go home". Champa reiterates this: "Madam, do as she says. Go home to your husband" (35).

Uma attends Minister Sharma's son's wedding along with her husband. Mr. Sharma being a clever person tries to humour Uma with flattery. He asks Uma what she searches for and tells her that he sees a spiritual quest in her eyes. This is how the conversation goes:

> Uma. And is that what you see in me?
>
> Mr. Sharma. Yes, I see a search for the truth.

Uma. Do you think I will find it?

Mr. Sharma. If you look in the right place.

Uma. Which would be?

Mr. Sharma. You know the saying about the Musk deer? He searches everywhere for the source of the heavenly fragrance, not realizing it is contained within his own body. (*CP* 37)

As the marriage ceremony of Subbu, Mr. Sharma's son was in progress, the hijras—Champa, Anarkali—came to sing and dance. Champa said, "we will bless this marriage with our singing and dancing". Mr. Sharma got angry and asked them to leave. Suddenly there was a turn of events leading to the unfolding of mystery behind Kamla's death.

When Subbu was shown the wedding photograph of his with Kamla by Anarkali, he demanded it. After he took it from Anarkali, he begin to cry and demanded his gun. Holding a gun Subbu cried as he made an outburst, 'you killed her' and then a gunshot was heard (he killed himself). After his death the whole picture became clear as to how and why Kamla was murdered. Anarkali who knew everything about Kamla's life and death told Uma the truth. This is how Dattani put it:

Uma. Why didn't you tell me?

Anarkali. Would you have believed me? Anyway, what is the use of all that? What does it matter who killed Kamla? She is dead.... So many times I warned her. First I thought Salim was taking her for his own pleasure. When she told me about Subbu, madam, I tried to stop her. I fought with her. I scratched her face, hoping she will become ugly and Subbu will forget her. He wanted to marry her...I was there at their wedding.... She gave me that picture to show to Champa. I saw the men coming for her. I told her to run.... (*Cries for a while.*) Here, madam, take this.

Uma. What is it?

Anarkali. A special mantra is in the locket. Champa gave this to me for you. Wear it and you will be blessed with children.

Sister! May you and your family be happy! Now go away, and do not come here again. Please go, sister! (*CP* 40-41)

Uma took the wedding photograph of Subbu and Kamla to her house and showed it to her husband to convince him that the Minister was behind the murder of Kamla and the cause of Subbu's suicide. The conversation between Uma and her husband, Suresh makes the mystery behind Kamla's death clear. This is how the conversation goes:

Uma. The photograph was what Mr. Sharma was after. A Polaroid picture that Subbu and Kamla had taken soon after their private wedding in some remote temple.... A picture of Kamla as a beautiful bride smiling at Subbu with the wedding garland around him. The poojari probably didn't know that Kamla was not a woman. Of course, Mr. Sharma couldn't have it—totally unacceptable. So he arranged to have Kamla burned to death. But Salim had to tell him about the picture. Mr. Sharma simply had to have that picture. He sent Salim to threaten Anarkali and Champa.... He did get the picture eventually...after losing his son. What a price to pay! And now he will be arrested and tried for murder. (*CP* 41)

But Suresh was not convinced. He was interested in protecting the Minister but not punishing him. He told his senior officer that he knew the truth but would not act on it. His words, "Mr. Sharma's gratitude will be expressed in ways that will be, I am sure, more than adequate...", reveal his mind. It is an irony of situation that when his wife, Uma wanted the criminal to be brought to book, Suresh thought otherwise. The play ends with a note of pathos in the agonizing tone of Uma in the following words:

They know. Anarkali, Champa and all the hijra people knew who was behind the killing of Kamla. They have no voice.

> The case was hushed up and was not even reported in the newspapers. Champa was right. The police made no arrests. Subbu's suicide was written off as an accident. The photograph was destroyed. So were the lives of two young people. (*CP* 42)

This can be interpreted as a protest play against the injustice meted out to the downtrodden in the society. Dattani is questioning the age old belief of marriage being based on hetero-sexual relationship. He seems to say that homosexual and lesbian relationships being as natural as heterosexual relationship, same-sex marriage should be permitted in India. Laws should be made to this effect. Secondly, the plight of hijras in our society is deplorable. It is *an irony* of life that the hijras who are welcome on two occasions—one, at the time of marriage, and two, at the time of childbirth—to sing and dance, are themselves deprived of marriage and childbirth. Dattani has done a good job by introducing a new theme to Indian English drama. Conservatives and social activists should not turn a blind eye to reality. Since in real life, homosexual relationship is an accomplished fact, why can't it be a subject matter of play? This is what Dattani asks, though implicitly. He believes that since in real life there are left-handers, which is as natural as right-handers, homosexual relationship is as natural as heterosexual relationship. We have to accept the reality of life, however, painful that might be.

Dattani explores the same theme of same-sex love relationship in some of his other plays as well. That is why, before making an exploration of the next two plays, *The Swami and Winston* and *Uma and the Fairy Queen,* in which both Uma and Suresh appear, I would seek to interpret on a *Muggy Night in Mumbai,* the second play in Dattani's *Collected Plays* (2000) which deals with gay personalities. The play begins with a conversation between Kamlesh and the guard in Hindi. Dattani without translating their conversation into English, takes recourse to transliteration. Kamlesh orders refreshments for his friends and asks the guard to make necessary arrangements. Later on, Ed and Kiran come and begin to chat. Since they are engaged, Ed assures his fiance with soothing words, 'Relax, I can take care of you'. Then comes Sharad. He begins to chat with Kamlesh. They have homosexual relationship. Again Kamlesh has homosexual relationship with Prakash, who is none other than Ed.

Two questions come to our mind when we go through this play. One, is this play a true reflection of human behaviour in terms of same-sex relationship? Two, can 'gay themes of love' be a fit subject of contemporary drama? Dattani in course of his introduction to *Collected Plays* (2000) claims that his plays are the true reflection of the contemporary society. He writes:

> I am certain that my plays are a true reflection of my time, place and socio-economic background. (XV)

This view finds support in the following observations of John McRae with reference to the play, *On a Muggy Night in Mumbai.*

> And the themes of *On a Muggy Night* deserve to touch the whole of society and to be touched by it. It is not simply the first play in Indian theatre to handle openly gay themes of love, partnership, trust and betrayal. It is a play about how society creates patterns of behaviour and how easy it is for individuals to fall victim to the expectations society creates. (*CP* 45)

Since love is more in the mind than in the body, the attitude to sex varies from person to person. No doubt, society imposes restrictions on individuals as to how to gratify their sex. But individuals are individuals—they find a way out to fulfil their love and sex. Dattani knows this too well and hence, his characters go in their own ways. John McRae makes a pertinent observation in the following words:

> Of the characters, Sharad and Deepali are comfortable with their sexuality, and have different ways of being gay. Sharad is camp, flaunting; Deepali more restrained, perhaps more stable. Kamlesh is anguished, and Ed the most obvious victim of his own insecurities. Bunny, the TV actor is a rather more traditional Indian gay man—married (he would say happily) while publicly denying his own nature, and Ranjit has taken an easy way out by moving to Europe where he can 'be himself' more openly.

I would be banal to see these characters as in any way stereotypical. They are a carefully balanced range of individuals with a depth of experience that exceeds traditional expectations. They are brought together in such a way as to bring out the conflicts, repressions and past secrets which are assailing Kamlesh and Ed/Prakash in particular. The past relationship between Kamlesh and Prakash, and the new 'romance' between Ed and Kamlesh's sister Kiran are beautifully counterpoised until the revelation at the climax of the first act that Ed and Prakash are the same person—which always draws a gasp of astonishment from Audiences (*CP* 45-46).

Same-sex love could be as demanding as heterosexual love relationship. It also arouses jealousy. Take for instance, the following conversation between Sharad and Kamlesh:

Sharad. You know I still love you.

Kamlesh. (*in a matter-of-fact manner*). Then why did you walk out on me?

Sharad. You were relieved when I did.

Kamlesh. I am sorry....

Sharad. I knew it within a month of moving in with you....

Kamlesh. I tried, Sharad, I....

Sharad. You tried to love me, but....

Kamlesh. I wanted to love you, I tried for a whole year.

Sharad. But you couldn't.

Kamlesh. I do love you.

Sharad. Oh! Spare me the lies! You could never love anyone because you are still in love with Prakash! (*CP* 56)

As the conversation between Kamlesh and Sharad continues. Deepali drops in. She knows their relationship and makes a sarcastic comment: "I am all for the gay men's cause. Men deserve only men!" Deepali herself is a lesbian. The following conversation between Kamlesh and Deepali reveals their attitude to love:

Deepali. If you were a woman, we would be in love

Kamlesh. If you were a man, we would be in love.

Deepali. If we were heterosexual we would be married. (65)

Kamlesh reveals his secret and regrets his action of being gay before his friends and seeks Ranjit's help to get over his difficulties. On being told by Ranjit not to be emotional, he says:

> Please! I am afraid! I need your help! I need you all.... After Sharad went away—I decided that I didn't need anyone to live with me. I had my work. That should have been enough. It wasn't. I felt this void. The same feeling when three years ago, Prakash left me, I would have understood it if he had left me for another man, but he left me because he was ashamed of our relationship. It would have worked between us, but he was ashamed. I was very angry.... For the first time in my life, I wished I wasn't gay. (*CP* 68-69)

Kamlesh was depressed and nostalgic about his relationship with Prakash. He became sick. On the top of it is his sister, Kiran, who wants to marry Prakash. Dattani has depicted the same-sex love with frankness and boldness expected of a postmodern playwright. After Kamlesh and Sharad, Ranjit too admits that he is gay. This is how Dattani puts it:

Ranjit. Call me what you will. My English lover and I have been together for twelve years now. You lot will never be able to find a lover in this wretched country! (*CP* 71)

While these friends were discussing how to solve Kamlesh's problems, Kiran came in. She told them that she was going to marry Ed soon. She also told them why her first marriage failed. When she enquired about his brother Kamlesh's health, Deepali told her that he was being treated for depression.

In Act II, the scene changes and Prakash (Ed) enters into the stage. He meets Kamlesh in the park. They feel closer to each other in a lonely place and there is a nostalgic harking back to the past.

Ed. Come Closer...Closer.

Kamlesh. If only they could see how beautiful we are together. (*CP* 81)

All the friends—Kamlesh, Sharad, Bunny, Deepali and Ranjit—know the secrets of each other's private lives and same-sex love. Now that Ed is going to marry Kiran (Kamlesh's sister), Deepali threatens to show the photograph of Kamlesh and Ed in an objectionable pose to Kiran. That is because Deepali wants her to know the truth. Kamlesh feels that Ed has now become heterosexual. This is how the story moves:

> Kamlesh. He goes to Church every week now. They put him on to a psychiatrist. He believes his love for me was the work of the devil. Now the devil has left him.
>
> Sharad. Now the devil has put him on to your sister. I'll tell you that. Show her the photograph. Let her know who the devil is. (*CP* 85)

As Kamlesh's friends were busy planning how to tell the truth about Ed-Kamlesh relationship, Kiran entered the living room. They were puzzled to see her there. Then Ed also came in. Ed and Kamlesh had same-sex love relationship. Kamlesh seems to speak for the dramatist (Mahesh Dattani) when he asks: "If two men want to love one another, what's the harm?" (91). Ed reinforces it when he says, "Don't be so afraid of what people think of you". Since these characters are 'gay' they don't have any inhibitions about sexual life. Kiran gets disgusted with these characters and decides to leave. Her Act II comes to a close.

Act III begins with a 'wedding band', as Ranjit questions: "Why do people get married?" Since Sharad, Ranjit, Bunny, Kamlesh-all are for same sex love, they don't realize the value of marriage between heterosexuals. Since Ed has come out of this kind of predicament, he looks at the problem from a different angle. He tells his friends:

> Look at the wedding crowd! There are real men and women out there! You have to see them to know what I mean". (*CP* 99)

Some of the 'gay' persons in the play are bi-sexuals and some of them try to be heterosexuals. Sharad, a 'gay' wants to be heterosexual because he now understands the power of sex. Thus, he says,

> We-ell, let me see how I can put it. You see, being a heterosexual man—a real man, as Ed put it—I get everything. I get to be accepted—accepted by whom?—well, that marriage let down there for instance. I can have a wife, I can have children who will all adore me simply because I am a hetero—I beg your pardon—a real man. Now why would I want to give it all up? So what if I have to change a little? If I can be a real man, I can be king. Look at all the kings around you, look at all the male power they enjoy, trusting themselves on the world, all that penis power! Power with sex, power with muscle, power with size. Firing rockets, exploding nuclear bombs, if you can do it five times, I can do it six times and all that stuff, power, man! Power! (*CP* 101)

One thing is crystal clear. All the characters are honest to themselves and bold enough to confess their sexual exploitations and preferences as well. They, in course of time, try to understand their problems and come out with astounding disclosures. For example, Bunny makes a confession of his sexual life in the following words:

> I know. Just as the man whom my wife loves does not exist. I have denied a lot of things. The only people who know me—the real me—are present here in this room. And you all hate me for being such a hypocrite. The people who know me are the people who hate me. That is not such a nice feeling. I have tried to survive. In both worlds. And it seems I do not exist in either. I am sorry, Kiran, I lied to you as I have lied to the rest of the world. I said to you that I am a liberal-minded person. I am not them but I accept them. Actually it is they who are liberal-minded. They have accepted me in spite of my letting them down so badly. I deny them in public, but I want their love in private. I have never told anyone in so many words what I am telling you now—I am a gay man. (*CP* 102-03)

In the end Ed and Kiran's engagement breaks off. Each character in the play finally goes in search of his/her own identity and seeks to know what he/she has achieved or failed to achieve in life. Finally Sharad, speaking for himself, in a way sums up the feelings of all the characters in the following words:

I ask myself what I have got
And what I am and what I'm not. (*CP* 111)

In this play, Dattani examines the psychology of persons who are by nature 'gays' or 'bi-sexuals' and the desire on the part of some of them to turn heterosexual. This may seem to be an unusual theme in the Indian context. But in real life such characters do exist. Hence, Dattani has re-created the characters in their own situations. To see this play on stage is to feel how these characters turn their inside out. Dattani has hinted at the need for same-sex marriage in the Indian context.

Do the Needful, a family play, is built on the theme of 'gay' relationship and as a result the marital relationship is given a new twist to suit both the wife and the husband. This story though appears to be comical reminds us the abnormal behaviour of a young couple who are willing to pursue their pleasures independently outside marriage. Sally Avens has rightly analysed the play in "A Note on the Play" in the following words:

> In 1996 Mahesh Dattani was commissioned to write his first radio play for the BBC; the result was the somewhat unconventional 'romantic comedy', *Do the Needful.* Like all the best love stories, the hero and heroine end up getting married, but the road to marital bliss is full of the most unexpected twists and turns. For me, this was the joy of working on Mahesh's script: his writing, whilst taking on a conventional form and being readily accessible to an audience, never fails to challenge and surprise. And whilst the play may be set in India within the conventions of 'arranged marriages', its wider themes are universal. A British audience found it easy to empathize with a gay man being forced to live his life within the norms of a heterosexual society or a young woman eager to prove her independence and break free from her parents. (*Collected Plays* 115)

Responding to a matrimonial advertisement Mr. Chandrakant Patel and his wife come to Bangalore to see Lata Gowda, the daughter of Devraj Gowda and Prema Gowda for marriage to their son, Alpesh. The Gowdas are desperate to marry their daughter at the earliest. This is evident from their following conversations:

Prema Gowda. Do you think it will work with these Patel people?

Devraj Gowda. Who knows?

Prema Gowda. They seem desperate.

Devraj Gowda. We are desperate.

Prema Gowda. He is thirty-plus and divorced.

Devraj Gowda. She is twenty-four and notorious.

(*Collected Plays* 121)

Since it will be an inter-marriage the mother is apprehensive. And moreover, Alpesh is a divorcee. Devraj knows the nature of his daughter and therefore, wants her to get married—the sooner the better. The conversations between Patils and Gowdas reveal a good deal of things about the society in the present context.

Though Alpesh and Lata got married at the instance of their families, they never shared their bed. Lata is involved with a terrorist. Salim and Alpesh has homosexual relationship with Trilok. The title, "Do the Needful" is ironical but appropriate as Alpesh and Lata managed to go in their own way notwithstanding their marriage. This is a typical family play in which parents show their concern for their children's marriage. In India arranged marriage still continues to be the norm, in spite of our changed attitude to love and marriage in the face of globalisation. Love marriages are slowly getting the better of arranged marriages in India, as the joint family gives way to unitary family—thanks to the impact of the West and resultant independence of the younger generation in the matter of choosing their career and life patners. This play reminds us of the growing helplessness of the parents to control their children from going their own ways. The result is evident in the characters of Lata and Alpesh.

Thirty Days in September is also a family play on sexual guilt and obsession with sensual gratification. Mala, the protagonist and her mother Shanta were exploited physically by Mala's maternal uncle in their infancy. Later on Mala became physically vulnerable and sought the company of men for sensual gratification. Her mother did not stop her from doing this. In the meanwhile a young man Deepak came and proposed to Mala which the latter turned down. Mala's father had left her and her mother long ago. Mala holds her mother responsible for all that has happened to them. The play begins with Mala talking to an imagined counsellor which brings the dilemma in her mind to light. She says,

> I—I don't know how to begin.... Today is the 30th of September...2001 and my name is...I don't think I want to say my name...I am sorry.... I know it is all my fault really.... It must be. I must have asked for it.... It's not anybody's fault, except my own. Sometimes I wish that my mother.... (*Collected Plays* II 9)

Deepak comes to Shanta and tells her about what has gone wrong between Mala and him. He sincerely wants to marry her and Shanta too approves of it. But Mala has turned down the proposal in a rude manner. That is what Deepak tells Mala's mother, "Last week, I told her that she was the most intelligent, sensitive and dynamic woman. I had met, she just stared at me and said, "I have something to tell you. It is over. I don't want to continue with our relationship. She does not want to see me ever again" (*Collected Plays* II 14).

Shanta tries to console Deepak by saying that things would be all right and he need not worry about it. But she is not in a position to control her daughter. She has gone astray and what is more, she holds her mother responsible for this. Mala gives two reasons for her fall: one, the western values which extol permissiveness and two, her mother's inability to control her.

> I don't know why. I just don't understand.... Please don't ask me why I do it. It's just a game...not a game. No...it's...I know it's wrong. What I am doing is terribly wrong! But it means a lot to me. I like it. That is why I am a bad person. I have no character.... I suppose it's these Western values, I wish I were more traditional then I wouldn't behave like this...no, no, that's stupid, I know, that's very easy to put the blame elsewhere.... (*Listening to the* counsellor.) It has to end in a month's time. In fact, I like it best when I can time it so it lasts for thirty days. I even mark it on my calendar. After that, I have to—move on, if you know what I mean.... Well it means that it is no longer satisfying to me, and I don't

> mean the physical part of it, although that is usually the main attraction for me...not that I actually enjoy it when they are doing it to me...sometimes I do, with the right kind of people...the right kind of people are, let me see...usually older men thought not necessarily so, Deepak my fiance, is only a few years older to me...I think I like it—I don't know how to put it.... When they—sort of—you know—use me... (*Listening to the counsellor.*) I don't know. I can't explain it. The only person who can, who could have prevented all this is my mother. Sometimes I wish she would just tell me to stop. She could have prevented a lot from happening.... Here are all the names of people whom I have been with. And the outline...well I just wanted a line that would put them all together. But if you ask me, whose face I think it is—it must be my mother's. (*CP* II 18)

Mala is not interested in marriage but wants to mix with many a men to gratify her desire. She goes to a party and dances with a man (Ravi) who came with his fiance, Radhika. Mala encourages the man to take liberty with her. ("They dance for a while, with the man exploring her back more with his hand when it is away from Radhika's line of vision".) Then Mala tells him ('pleading, looking up at him to be kissed') "Do whatever you want with me, but take me with you now" (*CP* II 21).

When Mala returns home, Shanta pleads with her to marry Deepak which she turns down in a second. When Shanta insists on knowing why her daughter is angry with her, Mala reveals the past with anger and hatred for her mother.

> I am not talking about a bad dream! I am talking about the time when uncle Vinay would molest me. When I was seven. Then eight. Nine. Ten. Every vacation when we went to visit him or when he came to stay with us. You were busy in either the pooja room or the kitchen. I would go to papa and cry. Before I could even tell him why I was crying he would tell me to go to you. You always fed me and—and you never said it but I knew what you were saying to me without words. That I should eat well and go to sleep and the pain will go away. And, and—Oh God! It did go away. But it comes back. It didn't go away forever! (*CP* II 25-26)

Shanta on the other hand, was of the impression that it was Mala who forced her uncle to do so. That is why, she was silent all these years. In Act II, Mala reveals that she has slept with many a men—not just the men in the office but his uncle and cousin as well.

> Mala also holds her mother responsible for her father leaving them. She says: "He left because of you. You didn't love him. The only reason you shared my room was because you didn't want to sleep with him.... He said to me 'I married a frozen woman'. A frozen woman. So don't try to tell me that you were concerned about me by hiding the truth. The only truth you want to hide is your failure as a wife and a mother." (*CP* II 35-36)

As Shanta gets moved by these words of her daughter and makes herself ready to reveal her secrets, Mala brings more events of her life to light by pointing out the accusing finger towards her mother.

> Mala (to Shanta). Where were you when he locked the door to your bedroom while I was napping in there? Where were you during those fifteen minutes when he was destroying my soul? Fifteen minutes every day of my summer holidays, add them up. Fifteen minutes multiplied by thirty or thirty-one or whatever. That's how long or how little it took for you to send me to hell for the rest of my life! Surely you must have known, Ma. (*CP* II 53)

This is the last straw in the camel's back. Shanta reveals her secrets by saying how the same man (her brother) exploited her physically and psychologically when she was six and continued it for ten years. Her tongue was tied because of this. Now Mala melts down and consoles the mother. When the secrets are revealed the mother and the daughter come closer to each other. Mala feels guilty of psychologically torturing her mother and begs her forgiveness.

> It's not your fault mother. Just as it wasn't my fault. Please tell me that you've forgiven me for blaming you. Please tell me that...I know you will, mother. I know you have. (*CP* II 58)

The wheel has turned a full circle and the daughter and the mother are united in love through grief and repentance. This is a family play in which incestuous relationship ruins the lives of girls in their puberty and young women at tender age. Mala and Shanta are victims of such outrageous relationship. Morality is thrown into the wind. Dattani explores a dark area in our social and family life with insight. His play reminds us of a changing society under the impact of globalisation.

Mango Souffle was adopted from *On a Muggy Night in Mumbai* and was made a film by shifting the location of the play from an apartment in Mumbai to a farm house in Bangalore. The cast remains the same and so also the theme. As Asha Kuthari Choudhuri rightly puts it:

> In *Mango Souffle,* the episode is more understated. Ed evokes nostalgia and memories of the past through flashbacks, to remind Kamlesh of their first meeting and his earlier contemplation of suicide. As he narrates the past, he tips his glass over the edge of the table, suggesting this recurrent idea in his present state of Mind. *On a Muggy Night in Mumbai* is a grittier version of urban reality than *Mango Souffle,* with Kamlesh's flat located in the chaos of the city (albeit typifying 'privileged' spaces situated in Marine Drive). *Souffle* alters this, and the action is located at a harmless corporeal, cognitive and affected distance from the city in a mango orchard. There is even in the play, the element of separation in terms of spatial reality: the plot unravels on the top floor flat that looks down at the 'normal' wedding—which is set at a 'safe' distance, which is also evoked in the film, once they are within the precincts of the farm. The firm in a sense actually makes the 'other', the outside, palpably visual, which cuts of the marriage next door. This is the subtle way in which the translation into the cinematic version evolves: this is a narrative that entails different space-time complexities, and the resonant emotional quotient that works wonderfully on stage would be completely static on the screen. (119-20)

Apart from showing homosexual and lesbian relations, these characters reveal two important things. First, women want to make an assertion of their femininity and therefore Deepali says, "Every time I menstruate I thank God I am a woman". Sharad was bold enough to tell Kiran, "No, I am not bisexual. I am as gay as a goose". Having said so, he emphasizes the power of sex in the following speech:

> You see, being a heterosexual man—a real man as Ed put it—I get everything.... If I can be a real man I can be king. Look at all the Kings around you, look at all the male power they enjoy, thrusting themselves on to the world, all that penis power! Power with sex, power with muscle, power with size...power, man! Power! (*CP* II 217)

This is a play about the hidden desires of men and women who want to confine their love to the persons of the same sex. This is as natural as heterosexual love and there should be no illusion about it.

Dattani's plays have variety and social relevance. If he has written about love and sex, he has also written on human compassion, music, dance and family relationships. *Ek Alag Mausam* (A Different Season) is about the HIV positive patients and the reaction of the people and society to the diseased persons. Aparna, the protagonist of the play is a HIV positive which she got through her contact with her husband, Suresh. George, a truck driver is a HIV positive which he got through the transfusion of blood from his friend, Joseph, Dr. Machado's son. Dr. Machado is running a charity hospital, Jeevan Jyoti in memory of his son. Rita is a HIV positive and a prostitute and Paro is her daughter. Aparna looks after Paro after Rita's death. George falls in love with Aparna and proposes to her which she declines. Manoj is another HIV positive who undergoes a dental operation hiding the disease from the doctor. People react differently to HIV positives (AIDs patients). If Aparna's mother loves and supports her daughter, George's father asks him to go away from his house. The society looks down upon AIDs patients. The play ends with Dr. Machado's address to the school where Paro gets admitted. This is a heart touching and moving play on the latest dreaded disease in the world.

Let us examine in detail how Dattani works out this story in course of the play. Aparna, the protagonist of the play, who thought to be pregnant was told by Dr. Sanyal, the Gynaecologist and the Nurse, Rosalynd Cooper that she was a HIV positive. Aparna reacts violently:

> It just can't be! I haven't heard a sexual relation with any one but my husband. I haven't had any blood transfusions, I always make sure the doctor uses a disposable syringe.... No, it can't be. Is not there a different kind of test? That's more accurate. (*CP* II 479)

But Dr. Sanyal sets things at rest by saying, "It is very clear to me that you got it from your husband". Dattani explains through the conversations among the characters how HIV spreads in the society.

> George. So to conclude.... Can HIV be spread through touch?
>
> Manoj and Shyamu (*forming a chorus*). No!
>
> George. Can HIV spread through mosquitoes and flies?
>
> Manoj and Shyamu. No!
>
> George. Can HIV spread through living, eating, sleeping with an infected person?
>
> Manoj and Shyamu. No!
>
> George. Then how can you get infected?
>
> Manoj and Shyamu. Through unprotected sex with a man or woman.
>
> George. Any other way?
>
> Manoj and Shyamu. Through infected blood and contaminated infected needles.
>
> George. Any other way?
>
> Manoj and Shyamu. From infected mother to new born.
>
> George. Any other way?
>
> Manoj and Shyamu. No. (*CP* II 525)

The society's reaction to HIV positives is shown through a conversation between George (the truck driver) and his father. What is shocking is the attitude of a father to his HIV positive son. Let's examine the following speech:

George's Father. You may live for another seven years. But you have killed us before we have entered our graves. What face do we have left in this village? (with great effort.) Don't come back. Leave. Go George! (Making a gesture as if to a beggar.) Go! (*CP* II 537)

This shows the real nature of man who can't think of any other person when his own existence is threatened. Philosophically speaking no human relationship is permanent—not even the parent-child relationship—everything changes with time. This is the lesson of life.

Aparna with a heavy heart filled with anguish expresses her feelings of being let down by the society. She says,

> On World Aids Day we remember those whom we loved but have left us because of Aids. All of us here today on stage are people who have lost their loved ones to Aids or will leave loved ones behind in this world because of Aids. (Looking out to George who is right at the back) I too am living with the fear of losing someone whom I love. And I too am not ashamed to say in public, am infected with the virus. (*CP*, II, 547)

This is a play of human compassion and the message is loud and clear in the concluding lines of the play told by the doctor who lost his son to Aids. This is how Dr. Machado urges upon the people to treat the HIV positives with sympathy and understanding.

> On World Aids Day, let us remember the lives of those who died of the virus and respect the dignity of those who are living with HIV. Today's enemy is not other human beings from another country or people of another religion or race. The real enemy today is a tiny invisible creature—a virus. The Aids virus knows no barriers of caste, creed, religion, age, gender, race. It is not prejudice, fear or ignorance that will win the battle against Aids. But understanding, precaution and above all love. Today the world over doctors and scientists are trying to find a cure for Aids. In the interest of

mankind we hope they succeed. While waiting for that cure to be invented or discovered, let us not forget—that miracles are known to happen. (*CP* II 556-7)

Ek Alag Mausam is a commissioned play. It aims at making the people conscious of the dreaded disease, Aids (HIV positive). It is the cause that the playwright is determined to vindicate. But it should be done within the ambit of literature without being didactic. Dattani succeeds in conveying the consequences of this disease through his characters who appear to be convincing. There in lies the merit of this play.

Dattani deals with a new theme in *The Swami and Winston* where people cheat in the name of religion and philosophy. Religious fundamentalism in any form is harmful to the society, for it strikes at the roots of humanity. Lady Montefiore, a rich woman from the West comes to India with her dog, Winston in search of her brother who is living in an Ashram in Karnataka. She is murdered and the suspicion falls on her brother and finally the mystery of her murder is solved. Pseudo-scholars and pseudo-religious minded persons are exposed in the end.

The play is an indirect attack on religious fundamentalists who use religion as a ploy to further their self-interest. Researcher Uma, the wife of Police Superintendent, Suresh and the daughter-in-law of Mr. Rao, the Deputy Commissioner of Police, unravels the mystery of the murder of Lady Montefiore. In the end, Swami and Charles Montefiore are exonerated. Constable Munswamy helps Uma in her investigation and finally gets a reward of five thousand pound cheque for looking after the dog, Winston.

As the play opens, Lady Montefiore goes in search of her brother by hiring a taxi. Her dog, Winston runs away and is found. On the way the fan belt of the taxi is broken and the driver goes in search of a mechanic. In the meantime something has happened and Lady Montefiore is found dead inside 'her car somewhere on Whitefield road'. Uma breaks the news to her husband Suresh and wants to accompany him to the spot, which he declines. This is how the conversation goes on:

Uma. Can I go with you?

Suresh. What for?

Uma (*after a while*). Just to keep you company.

Suresh. Look. I know you think you are very clever at this after that hijra case....

Uma. No. I didn't mean....

Suresh. Let me finish. I don't like you interfering in my work, I don't interfere in your work do I?

Uma. (*speaking quickly to have her say before she is interrupted*). You did. You never let me complete my thesis!

Suresh. Sweetheart, let us be clear about this. Your Professor didn't like your work....

Uma. I couldn't submit....

Suresh. Hang on.

Uma. The full paper because....

Suresh. Let me finish. It's 1 a.m. and I don't want to argue with you. I didn't allow you to use the hijra murder because it was a sensitive case. Just listen...this is probably one of these robbery cases. She must have put up a fight so she got killed. Some of those Muslims in that area have been arrested before. They must have stopped the car.

Uma. How do you know?

Suresh. I haven't finished.

Uma. You never do! I just want to come because I met the lady once. She seemed a wonderful person and for this to happen to someone like her is....

Suresh. When did you meet her?

Uma. Tragic, to say the least. Oh I visited her once at her hotel. She wanted some help with her dog....

Suresh. Did Munswamy take you there?

Uma. No.

Suresh. Good. Because I don't want him helping you when he is supposed to be on duty. (*CP* II 296-97)

On Suresh's interrogation Charles Montefiore says, "she was my sister. I cannot believe it! I had to read about it in the paper this morning!" Charles also tells him about his plan of living in India permanently. "If I am to be a Hindu, I might as well live in India". And Maqsood, the driver, on interrogation by Uma denies that he had a hand in her death.

Driver. How can I help you? I don't know anything! I leave her for half an hour and when I come back. She is dead. In my car. Couldn't she die somewhere else? Why don't you help me also? My life is not important? (*CP* II 300)

Munswamy gives a clue to Uma when he says that the dog, Winston was found at 16th Cross, Lakshmi Nivas the house of Sitaram Trivedi, a north Indian Vaishnav Brahmin. It is Sitaram who married her daughter to Charles for money and killed his sister. The mystery was solved at the end.

This play, the second in the triology which I mentioned in the beginning of this chapter, presents Uma and her husband, Suresh as the researcher and Police Officer to investigate into the murder of Lady Montefiore, who solve the problem of the play by unraveling the mystery behind the murder. The play is about pseudo-religious persons who hoodwink the people in the name of religion. Fundamentalism-religious or otherwise, is unacceptable to the people and to the country. The message of the play is loud and clear.

Uma and the Fairy Queen presents an intricate situation involving persons belonging to three different countries—India, Pakistan and England. On the occasion of the celebration of Independence Day, the British Council is bringing a Shakespeare company to stage, *A Mid Summer Night's Dream*. Michael, the British actor and Nila's (the Pakistani actress) husband is to play the lead role. Suddenly the news of Michael's kidnapping comes and the whole scene changes. Uma, the Sociology scholar and wife of Suresh, the Superintendent of Police along with Liam, the British Officer take initiative to solve the mystery of Michael's kidnapping and then his murder. Nila, his wife is found to be guilty of her husband's murder. Let us see how the play unfolds before the audience.

When the play opens, Michael is seen to be taken away forcibly (which is only stage-managed) by some people. Then Nila calls on Liam, the British cultural ambassador. Michael tells Feroz to behave and the latter lets him go for the show. Suresh tells his wife, Uma to keep her hands off this case but she refuses to obey. This how the conversation between the wife and the husband goes:

Uma. I think there are people who trust me enough to assist me with information....

Suresh. Oh give me a break! Everyone likes a pretty face! Do you really think they respect your intelligence? Those foreign cops, and all those diplomats you seem to enjoy socializing with?

Uma. I am looking forward to the play tonight. Please don't spoil it for me.

Suresh. You fancy yourself to be a detective do you?

Uma. Keep your eye on the road, Suresh.

Suresh. From now on I am keeping an eye on you. No more sleuthing around, understand? (*CP* II 427)

Suresh is critical of the British Council which reminds us of colonial rule. He tells Uma rather angrily, "Bringing a Shakespeare company to mark our Independence Day! If you ask me, they only want to remind us that they ruled over us once" (*CP* II 428).

Liam meets Uma and tells her about the kidnapping of Michael and at her suggestion he is about to cancel the show blaming the failure of electricity, when Michael resurfaces dramatically. The show takes place. And immediately after the show a gun shot is heard. Liam announced the murder of Michael. The British foreign office restricts the British officials in forty-eight hours. As Uma puts it, "the relations between Pakistan, India and U.K. are at stake. This is the real issue". Uma takes pains to go to the roots of the matter. Nila Ahmed was a married woman, Mrs Nila Malik. She had a child not by her husband but by another person. Nila says, "I never hid anything from him. I told my husband that child was not his when I came to know. He was understanding and promised not to tell anyone" (*CP* II 462). After that she married Michael and when she wanted a divorce he refused. So she killed him. This is how she confessed her guilt.

Nila. I killed him.

Uma. Why?

Nila. I wanted a divorce and he would not give me one. I also inherit all his wealth. (*CP*, II, 461)

Nila's son Feroz reveals the true nature of his mother Nila to Uma and Liam in an outburst tinged with irony and pathos. He revealed the truth by stating clearly that his mother was a scarlet woman.

Apart from laying stress on the lustfulness of Nila, Dattani also depicts the agony of Uma who is childless. To Suresh's query, "would you be happier if we had children", Uma replies: "Don't know, Suresh. Happier? I really don't know". In this context, Jeremy Mortimer makes a pertinent comment:

> Uma Rao is intrigued by the whole affair, gets to know Nila, finds out that she's been married before and suspects that there's more to this than either political intrigue or marital problems. It seems to Uma as she tries to sleep through the long hot night, after her husband has once again been berating her because she has no children, that the clue lies somewhere in the play, and a certain line 'I do but leg a little changeling boy' goes round and round in her head. (*CP* II 421)

No wonder the play ends with a note: "Damned if you have children, and damned if you don't." This is a significant statement which means that one longs for a child, but if child behaves like Feroz, it is better not to have one.

Two things that account for the greatness of a playwright are variety in themes and technical virtuosity. Dattani has variety of themes and also technical competence. Since I am concerned with themes in this chapter, I would concentrate on his thematic variety. Not only does he write about love, violence and crime, he also writes about finer things of life: music and dance. *Dance Like a Man* and *Morning Raga* are two plays devoted to dance and music respectively.

Dance Like a Man is a play about dance as a profession as well as vocation. The basic question that perturbs the minds of the audience is that can a man take to dance as a profession? And it is linked with another question—that is, should a man allow his wife to practice dance at the cost of the family life. Jairaj allows his wife Ratna to practice her dance much against his father's (i.e. Amritlal's) wishes. Ratna too encourages her daughter Lata to dance. Lata tells her lover Vishwas about her grandfather who built that grand house and blamed his son Jairaj for being a dancer. But in spite of their differences, Jairaj always respected his father. Jairaj has a great attachment for that house built by his father and would not sell it under any circumstances. Lata makes this clear to Vishwas who suggested that the house should be sold, for it would fetch a large amount. Lata replies 'Are you crazy?' They have spent all their dancing lives here. Even before marriage, they practiced with the same guru under this very roof. Lata extracts a promise from Vishwas while talking about her parents and grandfather.

Lata. Vishwas, when we are married, you will let me come here to practice, won't you?

Vishwas. Of course Lata! (*CP* II 95-96)

Vishwas sees the books in Lata's house and intends to take out a splendid brocade shawl. Lata puts the record straight by saying that these things would not be given as dowry.

Vishwas. I am going to ask for this as dowry.

Lata. He won't give it to you.

Vishwas. Why n't?

Lata. Same reason why he won't sell the house. It belonged to my grandfather. (*CP* II 98)

The shawl was given to Amritlal Parekh as a present by the Maharaja of Mysore. That is why it is to be kept in tact. Changing the topic Vishwas asks Lata why she intends to be a dancer. People have no respect for dance and much less for a man who wants to be dancer. Referring to Jairaj, Vishwas asks:

"What does he do?" "He is a dancer". Yes. "But what does he do?" "He is...".

As the play proceeds, Ratna gets worried about her daughter's dance performance scheduled to be held that evening. Since it is about her making a career as a dancer, Ratna takes extra precaution for it. She tells her husband with excitement that, "Our daughter is giving a performance that will make her career and she is not going to have mirdangam playing for her. How do you expect her to give her best? How do you expect her to dance? What will be announced to the President of India if he comes? There will be no dance tonight? Tell all those foreign diplomats to go home?" (*CP* II 103).

Getting frustrated with the failure to get a mirdangam player for Lata, Ratna recalls her father-in-law's attitude to dance and quotes his views before her husband.

> Your father was right. Dance has brought us nowhere. It's his curse on us. Nothing seems worth it any more. You should have listened to him. He was right. We were never anything great, never will be, and nor will our daughter be anything but an average human being. (*CP* II 104)

She blames her husband for not leaving her father-in-law's house. "You stopped being a man for me the day you come back to this house...", she tells him and holds him responsible for not getting recognition in life. However, Lata pacifies her by saying, "Amma, don't worry. No matter what, I will dance at the festival. For you. I won't let you down, Amma. Ever" (*CP* II 106).

In a flashback, Jairaj recollects how he was stopped by his father to do rehearsal in his house and questioned why his guru was staying whole day in their house.

> Amritlal. I want this din to stop. I want your guruji out. I have some important people coming and I want those musicians out before they arrive. (*CP* II 115)

On being challenged by his son Jairaj about the dignity of dance, Amritlal says, "I have no objection to your reviving the art but I definitely do object to the people you are associating with" (*CP* II 119).

In a profession like dance and music, permissiveness is a common thing. Ratna accuses Chandrakala, her friend and a dancer having illicit relationship with Seshadri, a mridangist.

Jairaj. What do you mean he'll only give us a day's rehearsal? He can't be rehearsing with Chandrakala all the day for the rest of the days.

Ratna. When he is not rehearsing with her, he's sleeping with her. (*CP* II 127)

In a flashback, Ratna recalls her father-in-law questioning her for going to Chennai Amma's (a devdasi) house for learning the art of dancing. She was deeply moved by Chennai Amma's saying, "Let the Divine in you be possessed by the spirit of dance. And if the two meet, you will be transported to another world taking your audience with you" (*CP* II 134).

Amritlal was unhappy with his son, Jairaj because he looked odd as a dancer. That is why he wanted his daughter-in-law to help him to look like a man. He tells Ratna, "A woman in a man's world may be considered being progressive. But a man in a woman's world is pathetic" (*CP* II 140).

While pursuing a career for her daughter, Lata, Ratna gradually drifts away from her husband Jairaj. Amritlal plays a crucial role in making Ratna independent with an intention of putting Jairaj in his own place. He allows both the wife and the husband (his daughter-in-law and son) to do their dance practice and performance, knowing fully well that his daughter-in-law will beat his son hollow.

When Lata's performance was widely reported in the newspapers and media, Vishwas became happy but Jairaj and Ratna drifted apart. This is how the parents react to the reviews of Lata's performance.

Jairaj. Have you read the reviews?

Ratna. Not all of them, not yet....

Jairaj. Weren't you interested in knowing what kind of reviews....

Ratna. I know what kind of reviews she got....

Jairaj. You have not even looked....

Ratna. (Shouting) I heard. Rave reviews! The star of the festival! The dancer of the decade! And why shouldn't she get reviews like these? I deserved it.

Spending sleepless nights arranging things. Sweet-talking the critics. My hard work has paid off, hasn't it? Hasn't it? (*CP* II 153)

In a flashback, Jairaj recalls how he and his wife moved in different directions. In the present situation he looks after his little son, Shankar and Ratna keeps herself busy with her programmes. Ratna advises Jairaj to do something else. Dattani brings out the misunderstanding between the wife and husband in the following conversations:

Ratna. Do something. Do anything....

Jairaj. Do anything but be a dancer. Do something useful like choreographing items for you, or playing the flute.

Ratna. You're not even good at that any more.

Jairaj. Whose fault is that? Whose fault is that only you get invitations to dance?

Ratna. Not mine.

Jairaj. For one whole year I didn't dance—turning down offers because I didn't want to dance alone.

Ratna. I didn't ask for such a sacrifice. Tell me what you want. I'll do anything....

Jairaj. I want you to give me back...give me back my self-esteem.

Ratna. When did I ever take it?

Jairaj. Bit by bit. Insisting on top billing in all our programmes. Making me dance my weakest items. Focusing the entire show....

Ratna. Face it, Jairaj, it's me they want to see dancing.

Jairaj. A young, beautiful woman, yes.

Ratna. And you are jealous? What kind of man are you? (*CP* II 160-61).

Jairaj regrets that his father and wife have joined hands to ruin him as a dancer. Finally, Ratna realizes that her son was badly nourished by the ayah. Ratna moves to the library and imagines her younger days dancing with Jairaj. The play ends with Ratna's thought, "Then we had all the grace, all the brilliance, all the magic to dance like gods" (*CP* II 165). This is a very significant statement. It means that gods have perfected dance as an art form. And Lord Shiva is the perfect dancer. The message of the play is loud and clear.

Morning Raga is another play on the theme of music—carnatic music. Like the earlier play, *Dance Like a Man,* here also we find opposition to music. The play is built against the backdrop of Vaishnavi's death in a bus accident for which Swarnalatha holds herself responsible and regrets this all through her life. As irony would have it, Vaishnavi's son Abhinay becomes a lover of music and tries to promote carnatic music much against the wish of his father. Abhinay comes to village after three years to tell his father that he is going to start a music group of enquires about his mother's violin (Where's amma's violin's?). The father expresses his inability to locate the person who has taken the violin. Abhinay gets upset about it and makes an attempt to meet Swarnalatha.

In the meanwhile Pinkie comes in a car and narrowly escapes an accident on the bridge. Abhinay and Pinkie meet and try to know each other. On hearing Abhinay's plan to start a music group, Pinkie offers to sing for his group. She has just come out of college and wants to sing in a music group.

Abhinay's musical party gave a performance at a banquet hall. The Manager made the payment, though he did not like the music. When Abhinay asked the Manager how he liked it, the latter replied in the negative. He was very harsh and outspoken when he said:

> There are hundreds, thousands of young musicians in this city and they all think they are different or unique, but they are not...you are one of them. (*CP* II 363)

Pinkie's mother, Mrs Kapoor wants to see her daughter as a musician—to be precise, a good singer in the same way as Ratna wants to build her daughter, Lata as a dancer in *Dance Like a Man.* When Pinkie asks about her father, Mrs Kapoor tells her that being a drunkard he was responsible for his death. Like Mala and Shanta in *Thirty Days in September,* Pinkie and Mrs

Kapoor come closer after clearing the cobwebs of misunderstanding.

Abhinay comes to Swarnalatha's house to thank her for sending him the violin of his mother. He is there not to blame her (as Swarnalatha thinks) for stealing his mother's violin and killing his mother but to ask her to sing for him. Being startled at the invitation, Swarnalata asks: "What do you mean?" and Abhinay answers candidly, "I am starting a music group and I want you to be a part of it." However, Swarnalata declines the offer.

A little later Abhinay introduces Pinkie and Balaji to Swarnalata and requests her to sing for him in his music group. This is how the play goes:

Swarnalatha. I don't need to listen to your music. You please tell me when to start.

Abhinay. Okay. You can come in after the fifth bar.

Swarnalatha. Hmm. Which raga are you playing?

Abhinay. Right. Good question. Which raga would you like to sing in?
(*Swarnalatha looks at him warily. She opens a book that she has with her, putting on her reading glasses.*)

Swarnalatha. You must always start with a Ganesh sthotram. (*Looking at Balaji*) He is the God that will remove all your obstacles.

(*To Abhinay*) Can you play in raga Todi?

Abhinay. Sure.
He plays the scale on his keyboard. Something like that?

Swarnalatha. Something like that. (Sighing.) Anyway, you play what you can. (*CP* II 376)

Abhinay requests Swarnalatha again to sing for him in a concert and almost compels her to accede to his request by reminding her of the past. "You must. I cannot do the concert without you". He reiterated: "Because it's me who is asking Vaishnavi's son. My mother played for you. You can sing for me. Or don't you want to return the favour because she is dead and it does not matter anymore?" (*CP* II 380).

Swarnalatha's husband Mr Shastri also persuades her to sing for Abhinay. On the other hand, Abhinay's father asks her not to help him in making music. He says rather bluntly, "Please leave him alone. Music will take him nowhere". The rest of the play, from this point centers around Swarnalatha who refuses to go to the town to sing for Abhinay. Finally, Swarnalatha comes to Abhinay's house and offers to teach him tala much to the surprise of Abhinay's father. Asking Abhinay to bring his mother's violin, Swarnalatha turns to Abhinay's father to say, "I can teach him raga. I can teach him tala. Let us see whether he has inherited some bhava from his mother."

Abhinaya father tells Swarnalatha that she is the cause of his son's degradation.

Abhinay's Father. They are laughing at my son, because of you!

Swarnalatha. They are laughing at your son today. Tomorrow they will salute him for his talents. But then he will be Vaishnavi's son. (*CP* II 403)

Gradually as the play advances, Swarnalatha and Abhinay become closer to each other and Pinkie contributed a lot to help them understand each other. Swarnalatha's guilt consciousness of putting Vaishnavi in the bus, which caused her death, haunts her without end. She grieves her friend's death more than she pines for her son. She tells Pinkie to go to the city with her blessings.

Finally, the show is arranged in the city. Pinkie tells Swarnalatha to fulfil her desire by singing in the city. The following dialogues between Pinkie and Swarnalatha make things crystal clear:

Pinkie. No wait! You gave up a lot for music. Now is your chance.

Swarnalatha. What do you mean?

Pinkie. The first number we play is called Morning Raga. It is the raga you wanted to sing. The one you taught me....

Swarnalatha. Thank you. It has been a difficult raga for me to learn. Twenty years is a long time. Music is a never ending journey.

Abhinay and Pinkie look on.

It has been my dream to sing for an audience such as you. But...tonight, I will sing this song for my son, who like my music, has returned after a very long journey. Abhinay, I sing this raga for you—my son (*CP* II 415-16).

The wishes of both Swarnalatha and Abhinay are fulfilled in the end. With the close of the play, "the wheel has turned a full circle" and the dreams come true. The closing lines of the play amply demonstrate the value of music and the difficulties in getting mastery over it. Truly speaking music is a never ending process. It's a divine art and therefore very difficult for human beings to achieve perfection in it. The title of the play is justified when Pinkie decided to begin her programme with 'Morning Raga'—a very important raga in music. Together with *Dance Like a Man, Morning Raga* establishes Dattani as a versatile playwright with variety in themes and insight into finer things of life.

Dattani has written some memorable radio plays like, *Clearing the Rubbles* and *The Tale of a Mother Feeding Her Child.* These plays deal with human misery caused by natural calamities like the earthquakes and droughts. Beneath these plays lies the social discrimination in the name of caste and religion, which arouses human sympathy and compassion for the victims. In *Clearing the Rubble,* the journalist Jeffrey goes to Kutch, a region in Gujarat to meet the boy Salim, whom he met a year ago during the devasting earthquake of 2001. He describes his experience to Nora in a letter while undertaking his journey to the place a year after the earthquake. From his letter it emerges that Fatima, Salim's mother and two of his sisters, Mumtaz and Saira suffered most because they were Muslims and also poor. There was discrimination against Muslims while giving relief to the earthquake victims. Jeffrey tells the relief-team that he would write against them for discriminating against minorities: "I am a journalist and I am writing on the communal and caste biased nature of your relief operations". Fatima recalls how her daughter was stripped in the hospital where she was working on false accusation of theft and how her husband and little child Saira died. She also thinks aloud how Salim run down the family in the school by hiding his caste. She tells Salim (in her thought):

> We are but speck of dust in this world of humanity. I know you are proud of yourself. But you were not proud of us. You told your friend that your father was a farmer.... You lied. You should have told them that you were a cobbler's son and your father was an honest man. But you betrayed him. I have to say something, Salim. Somehow I know you will hear my thoughts. (*CP* II 77)

And Salim replies to his mother in the following words:

> One day, there was a dead rat in the classroom. The smell was so strong that no one could enter the room. One of the children told the teacher that I should be sent in to pick up the rat and clean the room. I did not want to do it. The bigger boys called me a cobbler's son and said that it was my job to do these things. If I could touch the hide of a cow, I could pick up a dead rat. He did not say a word. Every day after that the boys would mock me, look at me with a smile, telling me that I didn't know my place. Nobody said anything or did anything to me. But they were thinking about it. A week before the earthquake, a new boy joined our school. He asked me what my father did when he was alive. I should have told him the truth, but for a while I wanted to be treated as an equal. I knew it wouldn't be long before he found out. But till then.... I asked him what his father did. He told me he was in town to work on a farm. They were farmers. I told him my father was a farmer too. (*CP* II 79)

Dattani takes a dig at the people and society for discriminating against the poor and the minorities. Religion and poverty should not be the cause of humiliation heaped on innocent people. In the end, Dattani shows the lacunae in the payment of compensation to the victims by the government. Salim tells Jeffrey about government compensation with a tone full of pathos and perhaps, tinged with irony:

> We stay on because our lives and deaths haven't been acknowledged. The government offers compensation to those who have lost their loved ones only if they can show proof that they lived and died. For those of us who were buried or cremated before a doctor could reach us, we have no proof that we did exist. It is not enough that my mother tells them 'I had three children, I lost them all.' It is not enough that our neighbours tell them. 'Yes I knew her children, they did exist!' The whole village can scream at them saying 'We did exist! We did live!' That is not enough. Jeffrey, I am sorry. I followed you. Outside my village I existed only in your mind. All of us, want to leave our mark behind. Even if only on a piece of paper in a government office, if not an impression on some unknown person's mind. That the ones we leave behind can say, yes I had a son, here is a proof! I lost two of my daughters, here is the proof! Proof that we existed!... Now that my mother has proof that we did live, and you know that we did live, I need not stay on. (*CP* II 82)

This play is in three voices with interior monologues. The poetry of this play is excellent and it adds to the charm and beauty of thought and language. For example, as a narrator Jeffrey writes:

> I realize that these people have lost their homes, their livelihood, their loved ones.... Everyone here has lost something or someone. They are not crying. There are no wails. Only silence. Grief everywhere but I cannot see it. Only shadows of people going about their nightly routine as if they were still in their homes with all their loved ones. Having their dinner or singing to their infants. Preparing for the night, as if the piles of rubble are a part of their lives. I walk past them all. (*CP* II 67-68)

Dattani is at his best in writing this poetic prose. Dattani's plays have variety and the treatment of subject matter is astonishingly original. He is equally at ease with different subjects like gay and lesbian relationships as well as music, dance and human compassion. Gender relationship in contemporary society, a hot subject for feminist critics, attracts his attention and he has given an excellent treatment of it in his play, *Tara*. In course of an interview he says,

> You can talk about feminism, because in a way that is accepted. But you can't talk about gay issues because that's not Indian, [that] doesn't happen here. You can't talk about a middle-class housewife fantasizing about having sex with the cook or actually having a sex life—that isn't Indian either—that's confrontational even if it is Indian. (Erin Mee, *CP* 319)

Honesty is the hallmark of Dattani's plays. He presented characters drawn from contemporary life and society as they are, but not as they should have been. *Tara,* as Erin Mee rightly points out:

> Centers on the emotional separation that grows between two conjoined twins following the discovery that their physical separation was manipulated by their mother and grandfather to favour the boy (Chandan) over the girl (Tara). Tara, a feisty girl who isn't given the opportunities given to her brother (although she may be smarter), eventually wastes away and died. Chandan escapes to London, changes his name to Dan, and attempts to repress the guilt he feels over his sister's death by living without a personal history. Woven into the play are issues of class and community, and the clash between traditional and modern lifestyles and values. (*CP* 319)

This play clearly shows the discrimination against girl child in the contemporary society. The conjoined twins Tara and Chandan had three legs between them but the major blood supply was from Tara's side. After operation Chandan got two legs and Tara one. But the second leg didn't suit Chandan and it had to be amputated. It was done at the behest of their mother. The girl child suffered and died. Though Chandan lived, he was haunted by guilt consciousness all through his life.

With the movement of the story, we are told that Chandan went to live in London, with his uncle Prafulla with an adopted name, Dan. Dan could not write his story without the story of Tara. He wrote to his father from London saying that he would not return to Bombay:

> It's just that I don't think I can face life there any more.... Tara has been dead for six years and now that Mummy has gone as well, there is nothing left for me to come back to.... (*CP* 372)

While trying to record his life story, Dan unconsciously brings the life of his sister to his story. He writes:

> Until I thought of her, as a subject matter for my next literary attempt. Or may be I didn't forget her. She was lying deep inside, out of reach.... (*CP* 324)

This play can be read as an example of how gender consciousness works both ways—first, as discrimination against the girl (here, Tara) and second, love and sympathy for her. Anita Myles makes a valid observation in the following lines:

> Mahesh Dattani dwells upon the fate of the girl child in a traditional set up. Roopa, a neighbour, narrates how Gujaratis would drown a baby girl in milk and later give out that the death was because the child choked with milk. Bharati, the mother of the twins, is torn between traditions and her motherly instincts to nurture the girl child in the best possible way. She is guilty of being a party to the initial surgery in which Tara unnecessarily lost a leg. She suffers a nervous breakdown due to guilt. At the same time she shows great affection to Tara by cuddling her, by bribing young girls in the neighbourhood to come and talk to her. When Chandan asks her if she has any plans for Tara, Bharati says,
>
> Yes. I plan for her happiness. I mean to give her all love and affection which I can give. It's what she deserves. Love can make up for a lot. (*CP* 349)

As a woman Bharati understands her daughter's needs; she knows that, unlike Chandan's, Tara's future will not be planned. So she tries to compensate by showering her love on the child. Bharati's concern for Tara's future is explicit in her statement:

> It's all right while she is young. It's all very cute and comfortable when she make witty remarks. But let her grow up. Yes, Chandan. The world will tolerate you. The world will accept you—but not her! Oh, the pain she is going to feel when she sees herself at eighteen or twenty. Thirty is unthinkable. And what about forty and fifty! Oh God! (*CP*, 348-49)

The age does not matter but the gender of the child does, more so when she is physically handicapped (58).

It is an irony of life that a woman (to be precise, a mother) should work against a daughter to favour a son. Feminism which seeks to bring gender equality to society unwittingly discriminates against women. But a brother's love for the sister transcends the gender bias.

Dan wants to forget his pain to function normally. That is why he says, "I forget Tara, I forget that I had a sister—with whom I had shared a body." Dattani closes the play with Dan seeking forgiveness from Tara. He says, "Forgive me Tara. Forgive me for making it my tragedy."

Dattani's family play, *Where There's a Will* shows the intricate male-female relationship in the family set up. Sita Raina makes an interesting observation on this aspect:

> Mahesh described it as the exorcism of the patriarchial code. Women—be it daughter-in-law, wife or mistress—are dependant on me and this play shows what happens when they are pushed to the edge. What interested me particularly was its philosophical twist. To be the watcher of one's self is to make intelligent changes in this life. In *Where There's a Will,* the protagonist has control over his family through his money and forges an opportunity to improve his interpersonal relationships. As do most of us. Consequently, when he became the watcher of his actions, he perceives that his desire for control has led him to be the victim of his own machinations unlike Kiran who uses power play to essentially improve her relationships. (*CP* 451)

The protagonist, Hasmukh Mehta being dissatisfied with his wife, Sonal, turned to Kiran Jhaveri, a married woman, who eventually became his mistress. This, he kept as a secret from the members of his family till his death. He too was dissatisfied with his son Ajit and daughter-in-law, Preeti who married Ajit only for money. Before his death, Hasmukh Mehta made a will, making Kiran Jhaveri as the trustee. His wife, son and daughter-in-law would get their maintenance only if they act as per the direction—of Kiran Jhaveri. This was too much for them to bear with. To add insult to injury, Kiran came to stay in their house. But here, the play took a turn. Kiran won the hearts of the members of the family by helping them. Sonal insisted on Kiran's staying in her room and Ajit realized his mistakes. Preeti was forgiven by Kiran for taking away Hasmukh's blood pressure medicine and keeping her vitamins in its place. The play has a happy ending with Sonal, Kiran, Ajit, and Preeti deciding to live together.

The play dives deep into human psychology. It examines the father-son relationship in which the father wants his son to follow his footprints and the son refusing to toe the line. This is how Dattani put it:

> Hasmukh. Should God permit me, I intent to stay right here. But everyone has to go sooner or later. I will retire one day, either from the company or from this world. What will become of you then? I have to season you now. You need seasoning.
>
> Ajit. Seasoning! What do you mean, seasoning? I'm not a block of wood!....
>
> Hasmukh. I should have prayed for a daughter. Yes, I want you to be me! What's wrong with being me?
>
> Ajit. And what becomes of me? The real me. I mean, if I am. You, then where am I? (*CP* 460-61)

The difference between Hasmukh and his son, Ajit comes out of generation gap and leads up to credibility gap. The desire of the father should not be imposed on the son. The mutual distrust between the father and the son has come 'a full circle'.

The play also reflects on the dissatisfied conjugal life, which prompts the protagonist to keep a mistress. Hasmukh was candid enough to admit it and in a way made an attempt to justify his action!

> Twenty-five years of marriage and I don't think she has ever enjoyed sex. Twenty-five years of marriage and I haven't enjoyed sex with her. So what does a man do? You tell me. I started eating out. Well, I had the money. I could afford to eat in fancy places. And what about my sex life? Well, I could afford that too. Those expensive ladies of the night in five star hotels! (*Smiles at some pleasant memories.*) Some of them were really...! I But that didn't go on for long. I mean, a man in my position has to be careful. I needed a safer relationship. Something between a wife and a pick-up. Yes. A mistress! It didn't take me very long to find her. She was right there in my office. (*CP* 473)

Kiran makes Sonal understand why the latter's husband turned to her. This is how she puts it:

> I managed, I managed my work, I managed my house, I managed my husband.
>
> Sonal. And mine too.
>
> Kiran. Yes, your husband. And your house too now. I suppose that is what he liked about me. I am an efficient manager. I guess I was...useful to him.
>
> ...He depended on me for everything. He thought he was the decision maker. But I was. He wanted me to run his life. Like his father had.... Even his attempts of ruling over you after his death through his will, are pathetic. The only reason he wanted to do that is because his father had ruled over his family. All his life he was merely being a good boy to his father.
>
> Sonal. How little I knew him. If I had understood him when he was alive, I would have died laughing. (*CP* 510)

This is a play about the understanding required of the members of the family to live together and happily. Kiran brings this understanding among the members of Hasmukh's family. Hence, the dead man wished:

> "I wish I had never interfered with their lives. They look quite happy together. With Kiran sitting in my place. Oh, I

wish I had been more...I wish I had lived" (*CP* 515). To a question, "how can a dead man exchange words with the living as in his e-mail reply to the present author", Dattani stated that, "in theatre, reconfiguring time, space and movement is where the art is".

Mahesh Dattani's best known play, *Final Solutions* (in three Acts) deals with the most talked about contemporary problem. That is, communal disharmony in India. The mutual distrust between two dominant communities—the Hindus and the Muslims—which led to the partition of the country in 1947, continues to be a thorn in the flesh of the nation even after independence. Alyque Padamsee's introduction to the play raises a few vital questions and unresolved issues. He writes, "the demons of communal hatred are not out on the street...they are lurking inside ourselves". He goes on to say, "can we shake off our prejudices or are they in our psyche like our genes? Will we even be free or even locked in combat...Arabs against Jews, whites against blacks, Hindus against Muslims? Are they any final solutions?" (*CP* 161).

The locale of the play is Ramnik's house and the central characters are his daughter Smita, wife, Aruna and mother, Hardika, besides himself and the two muslim boys Bobby and Javed who entered into his house during communal tension occasioned by the attack on the Rath Yatra procession. In the beginning Daksha recollects from her diary about the past when she was married at the age of fourteen. And now after forty years Daksha has become Hardika but her prejudice against the other community continues to be with her.

As the communal violence erupted following stone throwing at a procession, girls hostel was bombed. Smita heard about it and told her father, Ramnik to phone Tasneem's parents to tell them to come to take their daughter. To escape from the wrath of the mob, Javed and Bobby entered into Ramnik's house. The mob followed them to Ramnik's house and demanded that they be handed over to them but Ramnik refused to oblige them. This is how the dialogue goes:

Chorus All. We want those traitors!

Ramnik.	I have to protect them.
Bobby.	Thank you.
Javed.	Thank you. (*CP* 182-83)

Ramnik and his daughter Smita supported Bobby and Javed and gave them food and shelter. But Hardika and Aruna were sceptical about them. As the play advances it becomes clear that Bobby and Smita knew each other. That is why Smita has a soft corner for Bobby and his friend Javed. From their conversation it emerged that Javed played into the hands of interested parties who wanted to create trouble.

In course of dialogues with Javed and Bobby, Ramnik tries to impress upon the futility of violence which does good to no one. He also offers a job to Javed in his shop. But Javed is not convinced. Here are the exchanges between them:

Javed.	If I say I have changed, will you believe me? And what makes you think I want your job?
Ramnik.	Why do you distrust us?
Javed.	Do you trust us?
Ramnik.	I don't go about throwing stones!
Javed.	But you do something more violent. You provoke! You make me throw stones! Every time I look at you, my bile rises!
Ramnik (*angrily*).	Now you see provoking me! How dare you blame your violence on other people? It is in you! You have violence in your kind. Your kind is based on violence. Your faith is based.... (*Stops, but it is* too late.)
Javed.	Now say you don't provoke me!
Ramnik.	I'm sorry, I didn't mean....
Javed.	Oh. Don't be! That is the way you feel!
Ramnik (*shaken*)	Why must I defend myself to you? You are the criminal...no matter how much you attack me, you cannot justify your being a rio-rouser. (*Suddenly slaps Javed.*) You...you scum. If I had known what you were.... (*CP* 198)

Javed, as Bobby tells Ramnik became a fanatic because he was ill treated by persons of another faith and hired by the hooligans to spread communal violence. Aruna tries to save the situation when Javed wants to fill her puja water by saying:

> Please try to understand. We have nothing against you. It is only that, we have our ways and customs and...and...we are all equal. There is no doubt. We respect your religion and we wish you well. Why we have friends who are.... Smita has so many friends who are not.... All religion is one. Only the ways to God are many. (*CP* 209)

Smita tells her mother boldly in a straightforward manner about the superstitions prevalent in Hindu religion. Ramnik tells his mother that the owner of their shop was a Muslim and after an earlier riot, when he left, the shop was bought by Ramnik's father at half its price. That is why he wants to make amends for it by giving a job to Javed. Hardika tells her son why he kept it a secret from her. Ramnik answers, "you have to live with this shame for a few years now". The play ends with Hardika's regret for the past misunderstanding and change of heart.

But the play appears to be a little didactic particularly the dialogue between Smita and Aruna about their faith and form of worship. In a communal situation, only the liberal section of one religion speaks about reconciliation and criticize their own religion but people of another faith never find fault with the lacunae in their religion. That sounds hollow and the solutions hinted at in the end in the speech of Ramnik "If you call them they will come. But then again—if it is too late—they may not" seem to be too simplistic.

But Dattani takes a liberal, and we may say a rational attitude to the whole problem of communal divide in our country. In his e-mail to the present author he said, "It takes a great deal of confidence and courage to be self-critical. Being blind to one's failings is a weakness and not a matter of pride. If we as Hindus can criticize ourselves that should be seen as a virtue rather than a failing. Sweeping things under the carpet does not make a society grow or remain functional."

Bravely Fought the Queen (1991), says Michael Walling, "is a play about performance". It is in three Acts. Act I "The Women", Act II "The Man" and Act III "Free for All". The play centers round an Indian joint family with intricate relationship among its members. The world of women and the world of men clash with each other. Important characters in the play are Dolly, Lalitha, Alka, Baa, Jiten Trivedi and Nitin Trivedi.

As Dolly, Jiten's wife makes a plan after wearing the mask to go to an evening party, Lalitha, Sridhar's wife enters Dolly's room and says that she is there at Jiten's calling. Sridhar works for Jiten and handles Reva Tee account. Alka, Dolly's sister is married to Nitin, Jiten's brother. Dolly and Alka are not in best of their terms. Let's examine the following dialogues between two sisters:

Dolly. All right, I will say it! You're always implying that you have a better deal than me! (Mimics) Oh, didn't Jiten tell you that? Nitin told me a week ago! Or, Nitin told me all four of us were going but Jiten changed his mind!

Alka. But that's true! There is no need to imply anything, it's a fact! At parties, you just sit in a corner sipping your lime juice and speak when spoken to. You refuse to mix, you refuse to be interesting. You are just not...an interested party. That's why they don't take us out more often.

Dolly. Two years. It's not even two years since it happened, and you still want me to believe you have a better deal?

Alka. Don't bring that up! That has nothing to do with this! We are talking about socializing, so stick to that. (*CP* 247)

Three women, Dolly, Alka and Lalitha discuss the way they spend time and make comments on their husbands' attitude towards women in general. This is how Lalitha puts it:

> Sridhar says it is typical of women to do exactly the opposite of what their husbands want, just to prove they are independent. What do you think? (*CP* 252)

Act II is devoted to men and their activities. The scene shifts from the living room of Dolly and Jiten Trivedi to the office room of Jiten and Nitin Trivedi. Praful, their brother-in-law comes in. Jiten tells Nitin about Praful. Finally, the marriage between Nitin and Alka fails.

This is a play which dives deep into advertising products and improving the prospect of business in a world of cut throat competition and globalization of economy. Dattani makes things clear in the following dialogues:

Sridhar. I told you about the market survey. About a dozen women. A cross-section of upper-middle class, upper class and the stinking rich. We had given them a questionnaire each to fill up after seeing the AV. We needn't go through all of them. (Searches for them.) I had it all computed on one analysis chart. Where is it?

Nitin. Just tell us what they said.

Sridhar. I wanted to read out the detailed analysis. All my papers are mixed up!

Jiten. Sort them out tomorrow. Get on with it.

Sridhar. I can tell you what the bottom line was. They all said—in different words, of course but most of them used word to describe it—offensive. They all found it highly offensive.

Jiten. Bull.

Sridhar. I tried explaining to the directors today that women may not mean that they say, and in our experiences with various products, we've come across layers of complexities in consumer behaviour, and that this kind of survey had its limitations and may not work for all products. And this ad will appeal to latent subconscious desires and no overt, superficial, culturally-bound responses. (*CP* 274-75)

In Act III (Free for All), we find that Dattani seeks to bring a reconciliation between men and women. If Act I and Act II are to be taken as thesis, anti-thesis and then Act III brings, synthesis to the play, Asha Kuthari Chaudhuri makes a pertinent point when she says:

> When the two worlds converge violently in the last act, all the characters stand exposed, the sham and façade ripped apart. There are pointing fingers everywhere, the past and the future collapse into the present and the space of the stage is suddenly constricted and unable to accommodate the burden of the suddenly unloaded baggage. Dolly somehow emerges here as the strongest character, supporting a drunken Alka and roundly revealing the torturous truth about Daksha, Jiten, the aggressive oaf, is driven to guilty tears and he implicates Baa in his abuse of a pregnant wife before he finally drives off, crushing the old ragpicker in the driveway, to death. Sridhar, who has already revealed himself to be every bit as egotistical as Jiten seems now to don the mantle of the stereotypes as he prepares to leave with Lalitha. The play ends with Nitin finally revealing his 'gay' relationship with Praful, and the closing spotlight falls on the pitifully huddled figure of Alka in her drunken slumber before darkness envelopes the stage. (56-77)

Men and women seem to think differently. If men lay emphasis on business, women seek a way out to enjoy their life. What makes matters worse between them is the gay relationship among men. Men and women fell apart. It is another matter that they come to understanding with each other for the sake of family and children.

The Tale of a Mother Feeding Her Child was a commissioned short play to mark the six-hundredth death anniversary of Geoffrey Chaucer, the father of English poetry. It was "broadcast across BBC Radio 3 and 4 in the last week of October 2000", states Jeremy Mortimer in "A Note on the Play". To be exact, it was "first broadcast on 29 October 2000 at 6.30 p.m. on BBC Radio 3". Anna Gosweb, an English woman came to India for the second time after getting a letter from Jaman, a poor man from Gujarat, whom she met several years ago in Goa in her first visit to India. (It may be mentioned here that she bore him a daughter called Jennifer, who is now in the college.) Being affected by drought and helpless to maintain his family Jaman wrote to Anna:

> Dear Miss Anna Gosweb, I hope your God has been kind to you and favoured you with a good husband and many children. Our Gods have failed us.... I have never begged you or anyone else for anything in all my life. I cannot bear the humiliation any longer of seeing my wife and child suffer so. If you could send me a thousand rupees, I assure you I shall pay back as soon as we have a good harvest next year. Your friend in need. (*CP* II 566)

This letter was touching enough for Anna to come to India bringing all the cash (about four thousand pounds) in her bank account in the heat of Summer. Her journey to India has been described in a simple straightforward language in commensurate with her emotional attachment for Jaman. She says,

> I got on a plane and left for India...it was like stepping inside a furnace. I wanted to rush right back into the airport...the face of Jaman. Came back to me. I took the train to Gujarat...the air conditioning helped me sleep a little. I can't remember how long it look to get there—it seemed like forever. (*CP* II 566)

Having arrived at Kapileshwar, she came to Kapaswadi by bus and with great difficulty reached Jaman's house, only to learn that he was no more. She found Jaman's family in great distress due to acute poverty caused by drought. Jaman's wife was indifferent to her and in fact wanted her to leave. But her daughter, Shanti, aged fourteen took interest in her. On seeing Jennifer's photograph, Shanti said, "sister" which pleased Anna. Then Shanti fell ill and was about to die. Anna took courage and carried her over to the bus stop, asking her mother to follow her. She pushed passengers on the bus to make room for Shanti and her mother and threw a note 'must have been a hundred pounds' towards the driver to run quickly. At Kapileswar the volunteers rushed to their help and put Shanti 'on drops right away'. She was saved. Anna fed her, having grabbed the bowl from Shanti's mother. She says,

> I propped Shanti's headup on my bag and help a spoonful of the gruel close to her mouth. Her lips closed on the edge of the spoon and she sucked the liquid in slowly. I looked at her while she swallowed the gruel. Spoon after spoon. I felt-relieved. (*CP* II 571)

Anna stayed with Jaman's family for some months and enjoyed it. Her love for Jaman made her happy with his family and in his place. Her overpowering emotion is expressed in free flow of rhythmic prose in the following passage:

> I stayed on with them for months. I brought them food from the local sweet shop...we played in the sands, Shanti and I. Jaman's wife and aunt taught me some songs. They laughed at my Hindi. Soon the monsoons arrived. We danced in the rains...we ran through the fields and bathed in the pond. Mother Earth's breasts were swelling up once again with nourishment for her children. I could have stayed on forever. (*CP* 572)

Then came a call from Jennifer from the hospital and Anna had to go back. While leaving she expressed her happiness for saving Shanti's life and regretted Jennifer's attitude to her. She concluded her monologue with the following words:

> I am as helpless with Jennifer as Jaman's wife was with Shanti. There is a veil between us. But it is Jennifer who wears it. She can't see me, she can't see herself.... I hope somebody will save my Jennifer. By making her accept my help. She just won't eat. She just won't eat. At least I saved Shanti. (*CP* II 572)

This a play on human compassion which binds people across the world together irrespective of colour and race differences. It is the language of heart that makes communication easy among people belonging to different nations and countries and speaking different languages.

Dattani's plays deals with contemporary situations with a rare touch of honesty, sincerity and objectivity. He presents situations, and events authentically to re-create the characters as they are seen in the contemporary society. From hijras to homosexuals (lesbians), he moves on to portray the impact of dreaded disease (HIV positive) on our society. Again he portrays, music, dance, communal disharmony, family disruption and above all, human love and compassion vividly in his plays. His plays speak to us in our situation and we tend to see the reflection of his characters in our society. Dattani's themes strike us for two reasons—novelty and authenticity. There in lies his strength and the hallmark of his achievement.

WORKS CITED

Chaudhuri, Asha Kuthari, *Mahesh Dattani.* New Delhi: Foundation Books Pvt. Ltd., 2005.

Dattani, Mahesh. *Collected Plays.* New Delhi: Penguin Books, 2000.

———. *Collected Plays.* Vol. II. New Delhi: Penguin Books, 2005.

Mee, Erin. "A Note on the Play." *Tara. Collected Plays.* New Delhi: Penguin Books, 2000.

Mortimer, Jeremy. "A Note on the Play". *The Tale of a Mother Feeding her Child: Collected Plays.* Vol II. New Delhi: Penguin Books, 2005.

Myles, Anita. "The Subaltern Woman: A Critique of Mahesh Dattani's

Portrayal of Family in Mahesh Dattani's Plays

3

When writers of diaspora in the twentieth and early twenty-first century are in search of 'home' (imaginary or real), writers at home (which includes, poets, playwrights and fiction writers) seek to examine the disintegration of family resulting in the loss of 'home'.

Family is not only an important constituent of Indian society but the nerve center of Indian life. If Indian English poets and writers take 'family' as a metaphor in their works, Dattani examines the relationship among the members of the family with accuracy and authenticity. Marriage and the breaking of marriage, parent-child relationship, extra-marital relationship, difference in outlook among members of the family on various issues—all these attract Dattani's attention and shape his attitude to family life.

Love, marriage and man-woman relationship came within the orbit of family. The generation gap creates a kind of credibility gap which leads to misunderstanding between parents and children in a number of plays. In *Where There's a Will,* Dattani portrays Hasmukh's character authentically in relation to his wife, son and mistress. What could be the reaction of a father whose son has fallen short of his expectations, is shown vividly in Hasmukh's character. He says, "My son isn't really after my wealth. That's because he doesn't have any brains" (*Collected Plays* 456).

Ajit, his son has his own grievance against the father. He gives vent to his feelings in the following words:

> Ever since I am a boy, you have been running my life. Do this, do that or don't do that, do this. I was scared of you! Then, when I grew up, I learnt to answer you back. (*CP* 487)

It is not only the father-son relationship which was under strain, the husband-wife relationship was also in question. Hasmukh says,

> Then when I was twenty-one, the greatest tragedy of my life took place. I got married to my wife, Sonal. (*CP* 464)

That is because, Sonal was incapable of understanding her husband and also cold in love relationship with him. This makes Hasmukh says:

> I soon found out what a good-for-nothing she was. As good as mud. Ditto our sex life. Mud. Twenty-five years of marriage and I haven't enjoyed sex with her. So what does a man do? ...I needed a safer relationship. Something between a wife and a pick-up. Yes. A Mistress! (*CP* 473)

Hasmukh didn't love the members of his family nor did he trust them. But he had concern for them. That is why he took a mistress and created a Trust in her name to save his family from disintegrating. His intelligent daughter-in-law, Preeti understands him well. She says:

> The whole world is saying, 'Hasmukh Mehta didn't have faith in his own family. He didn't get along with his wife. His son is a spendthrift. His daughter-in-law is a scheming little witch. That is why he left all his wealth in the hands of an outsider! We have got to show them that he was...influenced. By this women. (*CP* 493)

Preeti is a new woman who wants freedom, money and hates the mother-in-law. She is very blunt and offensive in her manners. She tells her husband clearly and firmly about her mind in the following words:

> I will not take orders from you. I'm your wife, not your mistress! It's bad enough having your father's mistress running my life!... Oh! The two things I hate most in this house. The Will (i.e. Hasmukh's Will) and his mistress. Followed closely by your mother. (*CP* 561)

In a joint Hindu family the most intricate relationship is that of the mother-in-law and the daughter-in-law. They play hide and seek between them. Dattani rightly portrays such a relationship in this play. What is most important in a joint family is that who runs the house. Here, the deadman, Hasmukh controls his family through his Will made in the name of the mistress. The pleasant surprise in the play is that the widow of the dead and his mistress understand each other and decide to live together. This is an idealistic solution to the intricate family relationship. Dattani ends the play with a note of reconciliation between the members of the family and Kiran, Hasmukh's mistress:

Kiran. We all have to remain friends for another twenty-one years.

Sonal. Not for twenty-one years. Forever! (*CP* 515)

At this point, the dead Hasmukh enters into the play and stops at the door way.

Hasmukh. No, I don't think I can enter this house. It's not mine...any more. I wish I had never interfered with their lives. They look quite happy together. With Kiran sitting in my place. Oh, I wish I had been more...I wish I had lived. (Exists) (*CP* 515)

Uma, the researcher appears in three plays with her husband Suresh. The plays in which they appear are, *Seven Steps Around the Fire, The Swami and Winston* and *Uma and the Fairy Queen.* They are childless and that is why there is tension between them. If a marriage does not lead to procreation, it becomes a failure, wife and husband tend to suspect each other, though they may not come into the open. Dattani has dived deep into human nature to show the tension in the mind of Uma in two of the three plays mentioned above. Uma wants to complete her Ph.D. and take up a job to have an independent status. She tells as much to her Professor on phone:

Uma. Professor, this is Uma Rao! Do you have some time to discuss my paper? ...I am wondering whether I could leave out the case study on the hijras.... I know there is very little written about them...but I don't know.... How important is it?.... I guess I will have to...if my family throws me out, I hope that doctorate will come in handy.

("Seven Steps Around the Fire", *CP* 28-29)

Uma feels slighted by her husband berating her for she has no child. She too feels that the husband could be responsible for her barrenness. When Feroz disowns his mother, Nila, Uma understands the pangs of ingratitude on the part of a child. That is why she says, "Dammed if you have children and dammed if you don't" (*CP* II 467). Dattani closes his play "Uma and the Fairy Queen" with Uma's statement quoted above. He seems to reiterate the place of a woman in a family vis-à-vis her child. Not to have a child is painful but to have a thankless child is disastrous.

The tension between Uma and Suresh resurfaces again in *The Swami and Winston*. When Uma takes exception to Sitaram Trivedi's ways of doing things, Suresh seems to be sympathetic towards him. If Sitaram Trivedi wants 'to help the Hindu cause', Uma snubs him by saying, "You could have helped the Hindu cause by being a good Hindu yourself". Uma and Suresh discuss Sitaram Trivedi's onslaught on Charles and Uma herself in the following words:

Uma. ...by framing the Swami, he would get rid of an opposer. The Swami is truly spiritual and wants none of this new brand of Hinduism. Radha was totally under her father's control, it would be very easy for Sitaram Trivedi to manage the property once she inherits it from Charles whom I am sure he would have killed in a way to make it look like an accident. He had grand plans. England would have been the perfect place to set up his own pseudo ashram.

Suresh. Did this man Charles shoot at Sitaram?

Uma. Sitaram had the gun all along. He meant to kill us!

Suresh. You don't know that for sure.

Uma. Of course, I do. Why would he pull out a gun and shoot real bullets at us?

Suresh. In the court, I want you to say it was an accident.

Uma. That man tried to kill your wife!

Suresh. No, he did not. That's just your imagination. (*CP* II 325)

In *On a Muggy Night in Mumbai,* a play on gay and lesbian relationship, Ranjit asks a basic question in the opening line of Act III, "Why do people get married?" The answer is given by Bunny, "It is natural to the majority of the people". That is because heterosexual love leads to procreation. But this question and the answer to it can't be taken as authorial voice. In an e-mail reply to the present author, Dattani wrote, "you can be a nurturer and provider in a same sex marriage just as you can in an opposite sex marriage, procreation is a choice which some married couples don't exercise".

Contrary to what Dattani said, majority of people believe in heterosexual love in our society. That is what Ed tells Ranjit in the following words:

> Look around you. Look outside. Look at the wedding crowd! They are real men and women out there! You have to see them to know what I mean. But you don't want to. You don't want to. You don't want to look at the world outside this...this den of yours. All of you want to live in your own little bubble. (*CP* 99)

If family exists in heterosexual relationship in the society, it is the family which gives rise to incest causing mental harassment to youngsters as well as to the elders alike. In *Thirty Days in September*, Dattani protrays vividly the victims of incest through the characters of Mala and Shanta. It is not only Mala's story. It is also the story of Shanta as well. Both the daughter and the mother were abused by the same man, Vinaya (who is called 'Man' in the play), Mala's maternal uncle and Shanta's own brother. Mala's mind was preoccupied with the sexual abuses done to her by the uncle and therefore, she lost her inclination for marriage. Deepak, her lover who wants to marry her fails to understand this. The following dialogues between Mala and Deepak reveal the truth:

Deepak. (to Mala). It's over, done with, come with me. Right away.

Mala. You can't really understand me, if you feel it's all over and done with.

Deepak. What do you mean?

Mala. It can never be over. It won't work between us.

Deepak. For God's sake give me a chance and it will. For your own sake.

Mala. For your own sake, forget me... You don't understand! I cannot love you.

Deepak. Why?

Mala. (Looking at the man) because—because—How can I even begin to explain to you? I see this man everywhere. I can never be free of him. I am not so sure I want to be free of him. Even if I was, I am not sure whether I have the ability to love anyone...else. (*CP* II 53-54)

The agony in Mala's life grew because of Shanta's silence but she was helpless. She too was a victim of incest. Both mother and daughter are portrayed as pathetic characters and victims of a patriarchal society. Shanta's agony could melt stones if stones could be melted and her guilt conscience haunts her without end.

Freudian psychology explains the love between man and woman in terms of marriage, consummation leading to procreation and making of a 'home'. Lacanian psychology deals with identification of one with another—marriage or no marriage. If a man or woman fails to identity himself or herself with the spouse, marriage becomes hellish. Inspite of Deepak's proposal to marry her, Mala fails to identify herself with him because of her past experiences based on her maternal uncle's sexual exploitation. Hence, she refuses Deepak's proposal. Shanta, her mother fails to understand this. She too is a victim of her brother's incestuousness. Dattani dives deep into human nature and portrays his characters realistically. The problems presented in this play is unsurmountable.

Shanta tells Mala: You say I didn't help you. I could not help you. Same as you could not help me. Did you ever see the pain in my eyes? Nobody saw anything. Nobody said anything. Not my brother, not my parents. Only (*pointing to the Man*) he spoke. Only he spoke, only he said, only he saw.

The man backs away looking at Shanta with a warning.

Shanta. I was six, Mala. I was six. And he was thirteen... and it wasn't only summer holidays. For ten years! For ten years!! (*Pointing to the picture of God.*) I looked to Him. I didn't feel anything. I didn't feel pain, I didn't feel pleasure. I lost myself in Him. He helped me. He helped me. By taking away all feeling. No pain, no pleasure, only silence. Silence means Shanti, Shanti, But my tongue is cut off. No. No. It must fell off somewhere. I didn't use it, no. I cannot shout for help, I cannot say words of comfort, I cannot even speak about it. No I can't, I am dumb. (*CP* II 54-55)

Though incest threatens to break family, love helps to keep it intact. The union between mother and daughter in the end shows the triumph of love over depression and disintegration of family. Mala begs her mother's forgiveness. In his e-mail reply to the present author, Dattani wrote that when both Mala and Shanta realize that it wasn't each other's fault 'there is a true resolution to their conflict'. No wonder, the play ends with Mala's words:

Mala. While I accused you of not recognizing my pain, you never felt any anger at me for not recognizing yours. We were both struggling to survive but—I never acknowledged your struggle. Ma, no matter where I am, I always think of you. I want you to know that I am listening. Waiting for you to speak. I promise you, I will listen. I am waiting for a sign from you to say that you have forgiven me. Say something. Even a whisper.

The scrim wall around the prayer room rises. Mala is overjoyed. Shanta continues with her prayer. Mala walks up to her and kneels.

I just want to...I want to ask you whether you need my help. Please let me be of help. (*Gently turning her mother's face towards her.*) It's not your fault, mother. Just as it wasn't my fault. Please, tell me that you've forgiven me for blaming you. Please tell me that,

Shanta turns back to her God and continues with her prayer. Mala slowly rests her head in Shanta's lap.

Mala. I know you will, mother. I know you have.

Shanta picks up the bell and begins to ring it even as the lights fade out. (*CP* II 58)

It is the first generation's guilt that leads to the sufferings of the second generation. That is because the second generation is unable to protest. Dattani dives deep into human psyche and portrays characters with accuracy and authenticity. His characters—the victims of the social order evoke, a sense of empathy with the readers and the audience.

In a note to the play, *Bravely Fought the Queen*, Michael Walling observes:

> To Mahesh, a play is never really finished. Plays only really happen in the theatre, as ephemeral events. The apparently permanent printed text is just an approximation to what might occur when the piece is performed. (*CP* 229)

The theme of the play suggests that men and women enact hell between themselves if they fall apart. Asha Kuthari Chaudhuri makes a valid observation in the following lines:

> The play zeroes in on an Indian joint family, with the eldest male as the undisputable head, raising a gamut of questions on the nature of the relationships between the brothers and their wives (also sisters) and the manner in which identities form and firmly entrench themselves within these structures. Following some of the discussion on the family in the preceding chapters, we have noted the location to which the women are tied down, following the diktat of their men folk—they remain at home most of the time, with their chief duty being to care for the men's ageing mother, Baa. As the

> enclosed, cloistered female world of Act I clashes with the male world of wheeling and dealing, corruption and adultery of Act II, it becomes obvious that both the men and the women have assumed roles that ill-suit them, and hence all the characters have to seek solace in fantasy and the unreal. The veneer is ripped apart and the revelation is made as to the nature of their true selves in the confrontation of Act III, and the realities of their lives emerge. The braggart and wife-beater, Jiten is revealed to be another pathetic escapist and a weakling who literally runs away from the scene of confrontation in tears; Nitin's homosexuality becomes apparent in his revelations about Praful, the absent manipulator of the entire situation, and even the apparently 'correct' and 'sensitive' Sridhar shows himself to be one of the many male chauvinists in the play in his game of one-upmanship with Jiten. (84-85).

Lalitha, Dolly and Alka represent three types of women who seek to find their identity in a male-dominated world: Alka with alcohol, Dolly with her fantasizing about Kanhaiya and Lalitha with her obsession with bonsais, a metaphor Dattani uses for exploration of self and identity in trying to come to terms with reality that engulfs them. Lalitha emphasizes the impact of bonsai in the following lines:

> Oh, the bonsai.
>
> *Dolly enters from Baa's room and exists to her own.*
>
> (*Clears her throat.*) I suppose it comes with a bit of practice. In the beginning, you will have a lot of dead shoots on your hands. But then you learn and it...comes. Anyone can do it. You first find a sapling of your choice. It could be of any tree.
>
> *Dolly enters with her vanity bag. She comes down the stairs while Lalitha is speaking.*
>
> I myself prefer fruit-bearing tree because when they are fully-grown (*goggles*)—I guess you can't call them fully grown—but when, they've reached their (*demonstrates with her hands*) dwarfed maturity, they really look bizarre, with pea-sized mangoes or oranges!

Dolly enters on the sofa and removes her cosmetics from the bag. She has her back to the other two.

Anyway, then you plant the sapling in a shallow tray—you've got to make sure the roots don't have enough space to spread. You still have to keep trimming them as they grow. (*CP* 246)

The play can be interpreted from three angles: relationship between men and women, men and men, and finally women and women. Jiten's violence against his wife Dolly, at the instance of Baa which cripples her daughter, Daksha. Jiten, Nitin and Prafulla have intricate relationship. Jiten wants to take Prafulla's money and ill treated him afterwards. Ironically enough Nitin and Prafulla have homosexual relationship. Jiten makes it clear to Nitin in the following words:

I can take his (Praful's) money and still treat him like a crap. He is nothing. The very fact that he needs to show he is capable of helping us proves he is nothing. He is so inferior that he has to prove himself by loaning us ten lakhs! (*CP* 267)

Dolly and Alka married two brothers Jiten and Nitin and Praful their brother has homosexual relationship with Nitin. Baa is angry with her daughter-in-law, Dolly and Alka, and misbehaved both of them. It is at her instance, Jiten hits Dolly. The ancestry of Dolly's family has been personalized. Baa has taken them to task for that and asks her son to ill treat his wife.

Dolly. Fifteen years ago. Hardly married for a year. Praful comes to visit us. The same day, your mother receives a letter from her cousin in Ahmedabad. What fate! It had to be the same day! And it had to be that critical month for me! What was in that letter? Our whole history including the portion which Praful hadn't told you about.

Baa. Their father is not dead! Nitin, Jitu! They have lied to us!

Dolly. I didn't know. I didn't know he had told you he was dead!

Baa. Ask him! He is there in front of you! That cheat!

Nitin. The damage is done!

Dolly. Yes, we'd told our neighbours that. But you two were...marrying us. He should have told you the truth!

Baa. Read this letter, you liar! Your father is not dead!

Dolly. How were we to know he hadn't?

Baa. He is alive! Living with his wife and four children!

Dolly. My mother didn't know about his first wife till later. She was deceived too!

Baa. Your mother is a keep...a mistress! My sons have married the daughters of a whore! (*CP* 311)

The sons go along with their mother and ill treat their wives. This is a play where younger generation women suffer at the hands of their husbands and mothers-in-law. Jiten tells his brother to leave his wife, Alka. "Throw her out of the house. This time, for good. Damn Praful's money! The property is more important. You want to get even with profit? This is your chance. Say damn to his money and damn to his sister! Your marriage never worked. She is a drunkard. An alcoholic. Your wife is a boozer and you still keep her? What kind of a man are you?" (*CP* 290)

In spite of the humiliation heaped upon the two sisters, Dolly is sincere and courteous to Baa and therefore she takes Alka to task for the latter's bad manners:

Dolly. You insult your husband's mother in front of him and say you don't—you had planned it all!

Alka. No.

Dolly. You planned it! You waited for that chance of dinner time. You deliberately got drunk....

Alka. I wasn't....

Dolly. I could get that strong smell of mouthwash!

Alka. It wasn't that way.

Dolly. And you knew Baa would make those unpleasant remarks about our family to Praful and then you....

Alka. (*cuts in*). I didn't plan it....

Dolly. And then you say some nonsense. What was it you said to Baa? In that deliberate slur! 'Your sons are so different from one another. They are both petty like you, but otherwise ...' And then you wink at her and ask, 'Do they have different fathers?'

Alka. I didn't mean that....

Dolly. I know you didn't, but to say....

Alka. And I didn't plan it, for God's sake! I saw...I saw them staring at each other at the table. (*Pause.*) I can't forget what they did to me! Our brother is a cheat! He lied about our father to them. And he lied to me! He lied to me by not telling me.... (*CP* 256)

Dolly wants to maintain peace in the house. She was upset when Nitin threw out Alka for three months. She pleaded with her husband, Jiten to tell his brother to take her (Alka) back. But Nitin was furious. He made it clear to Baa.

> Praful tricked me into marrying her! If you want to hate anyone, have him. I have him now! Do what you want with the property but don't let him run my life! He is out to get us! Alka can stay here, or go away, or drink herself to death, I don't care. It does not make a difference to me! (*CP* 305)

This is a play on the intricate human relationship in the family and in the office. Jiten, the eldest son is not only a drunkard but a womanizer. He asks his employee, Sridhar to get a prostitute for him and Sridhar reacts violently saying, "a man has his tolerance limit, you know! And this is something...me pick up a woman for you!" Nitin is a homosexual like Praful and they have this kind of relationship between them. Baa was frustrated in her marriage and never loved her husband. In a soliloquy she unfolds her mind.

> It rained on my wedding day. He asked me before marrying him if I will sing! He knew that I could sing! You want me to sing only for you? (*Laughs.*) I will sing for everyone! Why are you so angry? Quickly—go away. Someone is coming! We must not see each other before the marriage, it is bad! But I saw. I saw him! He is dark! Dark! And I am so fair! My

> children will be dark, like him! (*Smiles*). Two sons! I have given you two sons! The younger one is beautiful, like my father!, He has my blood! Don't kiss him! You will leave tobacco on his cheek. Don't spit! Oh, the whole house smells of you! I have married such a villager! Aah! You slapped me? Never, never slap me. Nobody has hit me. The men in our family are decent. (*CP* 288)

Because of her frustration in life, she hated her daughter-in-law. But she has love for her granddaughter and wants Daksha to get to her house. She makes it clear to Nitin.

> Look! Look at Praful playing with her. My little Daksha! How happy she is with Praful. Look! This is the first time I've seen her smile! She is smiling at Praful! She is trying to get up to go to him! Oh, Praful loves my Daksha! Praful will look after her when I'm gone. (*CP* 305)

Dattani has shown in this play the unhappy mother-in-law and daughter-in-law relationship as prevalent in our society. In Hindu joint families they suspect and accuse each other leading to reversible reactions between them. Homosexuals hardly make their wives happy. Indirectly they do violence to their wives and their wives too never love them. This kind of relationship is shown in the characters of Nitin and Alka. Only Dolly remains good as a daughter-in-law and a woman because of her devotion to the deity. Dattani shows clearly how jointly family is breaking down in our society. All traditional values are thrown into the wind. Man and woman became individualistic, selfish and self-centred in the contemporary society. Norms of behaviour have changed. Like John Arden, Dattani writes 'kitchen sink' plays which make us aware of the contemporary reality. In fact, social realism is an important aspect of Dattani's plays.

If the broken homes upset us in some of Dattani's plays, he too takes care to portray human love outside family which reassures us that all is not lost in our times. Plays like "Morning Raga" and "The Tale of Mother Feeding Her Child" remind us of the women who can shower motherly love on others' children. Dattani has written about humanity with the keenness of an artist and insight of a psychologist. He examines human relationship steadily and sees it whole with compassion.

Three things that underlie the success of a play are language, setting and plot, action and activity. Dattani knows how to handle these three components well. What Kenneth Pickering says in *How to Study Modern Drama* regarding the success of a playwright is significant:

> All the modern dramatists who have achieved a degree of permanent success have been involved in the theatre, either as actors, as directors or as close associate of directors. They have often allowed their work to be shaped in rehearsal, have held firm views on acting-styles and have known how actors work. (90)

This is borne out clearly in the plays of Dattani because of his vast experience in stage direction. In "Morning Raga", Dattani clearly shows how the love of music transcends the barrier of family-ties and brings persons of different families closer and binds them together. In this play, Swarnalatha looks upon Abhinay, her friend Vaishnavi's son as her own because of his love of music. Abhinay disregards his father's advice and continues to pursue his interest in music. It is he who brings Swarnalatha to stage to sing a difficult raga, which she wanted to sing twenty years ago in the company of Abhinay's mother, Vaishnavi.

Twenty years ago Vaishnavi and Swarnlatha's four-year-old son die in a bus accident when they were going to perform in a town. After that Swarnalatha stopped performing. It is Abhinay, who after twenty years persuaded her to perform. That is because she looked upon him as her own son. This is how Dattani brings them closer:

> Mr Shastri (reading Abhinay's letter):
>
> You are wrong. There are forces that can bring back your son and my mother to us. I hope one day I can help you understand how proud your son would be if you sang for him. I don't know how to make you see that but I will keep trying. (*CP* II 411-12)

Dattani gives an apt stage direction:

Swarnalatha makes a decision. Swarnalatha walks towards the stage. Pinkie is relieved. Abhinay looks on. Swarnalatha touches the stage with her hand in salutation.

The lights go off and a follow spot comes on Swarnalatha. One stays on Pinkie as she gestures to Swarnalatha to take her place. Swarnalatha walks slowly to the mike. She looks at the audience. She is truly overwhelmed to be there. It is a dream come true. When she takes her place, Pinkie makes an announcement, Swarnalatha begins with the scale of raga Sindu, Bhairavi, going into intricate patterns. Rajeev sits up. Mrs. Kapoor is pleased. There is a warm applause to this. Swarnalatha is touched;

Swarnalatha. Thank you. It has been a difficult raga for me to learn. Twenty years is a long time. Music is a never ending journey.

Abhinay and Pinkie look on.

It has been my dream to sing for an audience such as you. But... (*Finding it difficult to get the words.*) tonight, I will sing this song for my son who, like my music, has returned after a very long journey. (*Looking of Abhinay!*) Abhinay, I sing this raga for you —my son. (*CP* II 416)

Dattani closes the play with a brilliant stage direction as follows:

Another spotlight picks up Abhinay who is so touched by this tribute. Swarnalatha begins to sing once again, Abhinay picks up his violin and begins to play. Pinkie joins in on the English lyrics. The three are lit in individual follow spots. Swarnalatha looks at Abhinay as he plays. A flashback of Swarnalatha imagining singing this song to her son. They are playing by the river. Abhinay when he plays the violin.... A flashback where Abhinay imagines his mother Vaishnavi singing and playing with him. Pinkie sings and imagines (flashback) her father rocking her to sleep. The three of them come together in one spot. Flashback of Swarnalatha and her son, Vaishnavi and young Abhinay, running in slow motion across the bridge. The song ends to a thunderous applause. They take their bows and look at each other. The music picks up as the credits roll.

> We see Rajeev enthralled by the performance. The villagers are whistling for Abhinay. Abhinay's father is touched. The villagers carrying Abhinay outside the auditorium. Swarnalatha and Pinkie embrace. Abhinay and Swarnalatha embrace controlling their tears. (*CP* II 416-17)

Music cements the human bond beyond the boundary of family. Love of music, and dance brings people of different families together. Passion for music, art and dance, arouses love in the heart of the people for each other who work in a group. It is a kind of love deeply rooted both in the heart and mind of a person surpassing the love for the opposite sex. Hence, it unites people of the same taste and goes beyond blood relationship. That is why Swarnalatha, Abhinay and Pinkie come together in "Morning Raga".

In *Dance Like a Man*, Dattani shows intricate family relationship in which the dancing couple Ratna and Jairaj learn and practice dance in their house disregarding Amritlal Parekh's advice not to do so. Not only that, Ratna also encourages their daughter, Lata to continue dancing and be a good dancer. In the end, Amritlal Parekh plays a trick on his son by encouraging his daughter-in-law to dance. The result is that the dancing couple, Ratna and Jairaj fall apart.

The conversation between the husband and wife turns bitter when Jairaj accuses his wife, Ratna of destroying him as a dancer. Dattani puts it very effectively in the following lines:

> Jairaj. Do anything but be a dancer. Do something useful like choreographing items for you, or playing the flute.
>
> Ratna. You're not even good at that any more.
>
> Jairaj. Whose fault is that? Whose fault is that only you get invitations to dance?
>
> Ratna. No mine.
>
> Jairaj. For one whole year I didn't dance—turning down offers because I didn't want to dance alone.
>
> Ratna. I didn't ask for such a sacrifice. Tell me what you want, I'll do anything....

Jairaj. I want you to give me back...give me back my self-esteem?

Ratna. When did I ever take it?

Jairaj. Bit my bit. Insisting on top billing in all our programmes. Making me dance my weakest items. Focusing the entire show....

Ratna. Face it, Jairaj, it's me they want to see dancing.

Jairaj. A young, beautiful woman, yes.

Ratna. And you are jealous? What kind of man are you?

Jairaj. Oh, you are clever. No wonder you get along well with him.

Ratna. Get along well with whom?

Jairaj. My father. It was him, wasn't it? (*CP* II 160-61)

This reminds us of the film "Abhimaan" where a singing couple (Cast: Amitabh Bachhan and Jaya) got estranged because the wife excelled the husband and the latter became jealous. Here, Dattani creates the same situation when Jairaj became jealous of Ratna and the latter underestimates (rather, looks down upon) the former. Love of profession and jealousy arising out of it, if not balanced properly, will lead to disastrous consequences as we see in the lives of Ratna and her husband, Jairaj.

The misunderstanding between Ratna and Jairaj deepens and she accuses her husband of destroying his own career, and family life. She goes to perform alone ignoring the husband. No wonder the family remains on the brink of disaster.

Dattani is a good observer of human beings in the profession of singing and dancing. That is why, in these two plays, *Morning Raga* and *Dance Like a Man* he has dived deep into the hearts of the characters to reveal their true feelings. Artists are sensitive people prone to jealousy. These fame hungry people can spoil the family relationship for the sake of profession. Dattani knows it too well.

In his radio play, *The Tale of a Mother Feeding Her Child*, Dattani portrays a character, Anna Gosweb, an English woman, who comes to a village in Gujarat to meet a local man with whom she had an affair some years back. Reaching that village, she finds an awkward situation in which the family of her lover, Jaman gets entangled with her. She succeeds in saving the life of Shanti, her lover's daughter. Like Hasmukh Mehta's keep, Kiran in *Where There's a Will*, Anna takes Jaman's family as her own. She would have stayed with them forever but for her daughter, Jennifer's call from the hospital. Anna narrates her feelings in the following words:

> I stayed on with them for months. I brought them food from the local sweet shop. Day after day we gorged on samosas, jalebis, kachoris...the whole hut was filled with bottles of mineral water. The postman visited us often and translated for us. We played in the sands, Shanti and I. Jaman's wife and aunt taught me some songs. They laughed at my Hindi. Soon the monsoons arrived. We danced in the rains. I helped them plough their land. We ran through the fields and bathed in the pond. Mother Earth's breasts were swelling up once again with nourishment for her children. I could have stayed on for ever. (*CP* II 572)

Love for individuals and concern for them, endears one to other human beings. Nationality and gender don't matter. Love triumphs all.

> Dattani shows how problems in the society rocks the family in "Final Solutions". Kenneth Pickering has rightly pointed out that social problems do affect us, our family relationship. As Pickering has rightly observed that "the problem play is that 'which explores a particular social problem, raising many questions about it and provoking the audience into finding answers. Such plays, sometimes known as, 'thesis plays' because they mount and workout an argument, may be tragic or comic in essence but their ideas constitute some issue of deep concern to the dramatist with which he wishes to engage the minds and consciences of the audience." (70)

Final Solutions is a problem play, for it deals with the communal tension of our society. The violence perpetuated by the communal people in our society affect family-life and that is dramatized in the characters of Smita, Ramnik Gandhi, Aruna,

Bobby and Javed. The same character Daksha with two names (Daksha and Hardika) shows how the attitude of the same person to communal tension has changed over the years. Two Muslim boys, Bobby and Javed take shelter in Ramnik's house during communal violence in the town. The dialogue between these two boys with the members of Ramnik's family reveals the deep-rooted distrust between two communities. Aruna, Ramnik's wife argues with her husband and daughter, Smita against giving them shelter in their house when Aruna forbids Bobby and Javed to touch the water with which she bathes the gods. She makes it clear to Smita:

> We bathe our gods with it, Smita. It has to be pure. It must not be contaminated.... What makes you think you have all the answers? Don't you have any respect for who you are? I shudder to think what will become of your children. What kind of sanskar will you give them when you don't have any yourself? It's all very well to have progressive ideas. But are you progressing or are you drifting? God knows, I don't want all this violence. How can I, when I won't even harm a goat or a chicken? But to throw everything away just like that? Doesn't it mean anything to you? For so many generations we have preserved our sanskar because we believe it is the truth! It is the way shown to us by our saints. We must know no other path. And I will not have it all perish to accommodate someone else's faith. I have enough faith and pride to see that it doesn't happen. I shall uphold what I believe is the truth. (*CP* 209-10)

Aruna's logic is not acceptable to her daughter, Smita. Here, is an instance of the younger generation differing from the older generation in the matters of faith. Mother and daughter show two different attitudes to religion: conservative and liberal. In matters of faith it is difficult to say which is right and which is wrong, or rational or irrational. Either one believes or does not believe in a faith. It is a matter of individual perception or belief. Hence, the daughter retorts the mother in the following words:

> Because you know they don't believe in all the things that you feel are true. Doesn't that make your belief that much more weak? Do two young boys make you so insecure?

> Come on, mummy. This is a time for strength! I am so glad these two dropped in. We would never have spoken about what makes us so different from each other. We would have gone on living our lives with our petty similarities. (*CP* 211)

Ramnik's candid confession that his father had burnt the Muslim shop in an earlier riot and took possession of it. He regretted this action and her mother being sensitive immediately agreed with her son. *Final Solutions,* at this point seem to be a reality.

When Ramnik explains to his mother Hardika the background of their gaining control over a shop, things become clear.

> Hardika. (*crushed*). Why didn't you tell me? All these years.
>
> Ramnik. You have to live with this shame only for a few years now.
>
> *Pause.*
>
> Hardika. Do you think...do you think those boys will ever come back?
>
> Ramnik. If you call them they will come. But then again—if it's too late—they may not. (*CP* 226)

The relationship among the members of Ramnik's family is affected by the communal feelings prevalent in our society. But Dattani works out a solution by making people understand the evil inherent in such kind of communal hatred between two major communities in our country.

If communal violence rocks the family relationship in *Final Solutions,* it is Aids, a fatal disease which upsets the family ties in *Ek Alag Mausam*. Aparna, Rita, Manoj and George are suffering from Aids and in the process, they are losing the sympathy of their families. Aparna refuses to marry George on this ground, but the latter insists on it.

> George. Forget for a moment that we are HIV. Forget that we have five, seven, ten, twelve years to live. Forget that and then think of our lives together.
>
> Aparna. How can I forget? It is there! Written in our medical reports. Our death warrant. We can have

those tests done over and over again but the truth is we will one day have Aids!

George. You have branded yourself Aids, Aids, Aids! You have put a big red stamp on yourself. I thought only an uncaring, unfeeling society would do that to us. But no. We don't have to worry about society. We are doing it to ourselves! I refuse to brand myself. All I know is that I love you and I want to marry you. (*CP* II 533)

What is ironic is that George's father asks him to get out of their village. He says,

> You may live for another seven years. But you have killed us before we have entered our graves. What face do we have left in this village? Don't come back. Leave. Go George! (Making a gesture as if to a beggar) Go! (*CP* II 537)

Family relationship breaks down when members of the family suffers from Aids. What a pity! Father disowns the son. How fragile is the family relationship?

The family relationship (i.e. the relationship among the members of the family) as portrayed in Dattani's plays is authentic and realistic in our situation. To read his plays and watch the characters enacting their roles, is to transport us to the everyday world in which we live. Such characters we encounter in our society—they are life-like and real. Therein lies Datani's strength as a dramatist. The disintegration in family-life is typical of Indian situation in the contemporary society. But there is a limitation in Dattani's plays. That is, the family portrayed in his plays is the urban family in our society. Rural life and family are not portrayed here. But then, rural family has also come under strain because of large scale migration to the town and the city. No longer the saying "heaven is where home is" holds good—either in rural India or in urban India. That's why Dattani's plays appeal to us in our situation and make us see into the rot, that has set in.

WORKS CITED

Chaudhuri, Asha Kuthari, *Mahesh Dattani*. New Delhi: Foundation Books Pvt. Ltd., 2005.

Dattani, Mahesh. *Collected Plays.* New Delhi: Penguin Books of India, 2000.

———. *Collected Plays*, Vol. II. New Delhi: Penguin Books India, 2005.

Pickering, Kenneth. *How to Study Modern Drama.* London: Macmillan, 1988.

Social Exclusion in Mahesh Dattani's Plays

4

Mahesh Dattani is the first and only one Indian English dramatist to win the Sahitya Akademi Award so far for his work, *Final Solutions* and *Other Plays* for 1998. He has two volumes of plays titled *Collected Plays* (2000) and *Collected Plays,* Vol. II (2005) in Penguin imprint. He has just completed a radio play, *The Girl Who Touched the Stars* for BBC Radio. Contemporary reality and society form the nerve center of his plays. He deals with the discriminations against people in our society on the basis of religion, class, gender and sexuality with insight and empathy. Here, an attempt has been made to show that the social exclusion in his plays calls for a radical reformation and a change of heart leading to individual as well as social transformation.

Social exclusion is a worldwide phenomenon. In a multilingual and multicultural country like India, it is a major problem that threatens the very fabric of our society. Factors like caste, religion, community and gender give rise to social exclusion. But social exclusion as a concept emerged in the last quarter of the twentieth century, though the Indian society witnessed this right from time immemorial when it was divided on the basis of caste. The upper caste hegemony was instrumental in causing the exclusion of the lower caste people from the rank of the society. Mahesh Dattani, the most significant Indian English playwright of our country deals with the theme of social exclusion in his plays not on the basis of caste but gender. How gender relationship based on sexuality causes social exclusion becomes a prime concern for him in some of his plays.

Neuter sexuality, gay relationship and disease with social stigma like Aids cause social exclusion in our country. This is a cause for concern in the contemporary society. Dattani depicts these themes deftly in "Seven Steps Around the Fire", "On a Muggy Night in Mumbai", "Do the Needful", "Mango Souffle", and "Ek Alag Mausam". "Seven Steps Around the Fire" was first broadcast as "Seven Circles Around the Fire" by BBC Radio 4 on 9 January 1999. This is a play about hijra community who suffer from social exclusion in our country. Dattani explains the term hijra through the mouth of the Researcher in Sociology, Uma by going to the origin of the myth in the *Ramayana.*

> A brief note on the popular myths on the origin of the hijras will be in order, before looking at the class-gender-based power implications. The term hijra, of course, is of Urdu origin, a combination of Hindi, Persian and Arabic, literally meaning 'neither male nor female'. Another legend traces their ancestry to *the Ramayana*. The legend has it that god Rama was going to cross the river and go into exile in the forest. All the people of the city wanted to follow him. He said, "Men and women, turn back'. Some of his male followers did not know what to do. They could not disobey him. So they sacrificed their masculinity, to become neither men nor women, and followed him to the forest. Rama was pleased with their devotion and blessed them. There are trans-sexuals all over the world, and India is no exception. The purpose of this case study is to show their position in society. Perceived as the lowest of the low, they yearn for family and love. The two events in mainstream Hindu culture where their presence is acceptable—marriage and birth—ironically are the very same privileges denied to them by man and nature. (*CP* 10-11)

A hijra named Kamala was secretly married to Subbu, the son of a Minister. She (i.e. Kamla) was burned to death at the behest of the Minister who hastily arranged a girl for marriage to his son. But at the wedding ceremony, which was attended by guests as well as hijras, Subbu brought out a gun and shot at himself. The suicide was hushed up. Uma, the researcher moving from pillar to post to find out the man behind Kamala's murder, meets other hijras like Anarkali and Champa and interrogates them. She thinks aloud about hijra community. Uma (thought):

> Nobody seems to know anything about them. Neither do they. Did they come to this country with Islam, or are they a part of our glorious Hindu tradition? Why are they so obsessed with weddings and ceremonies of childbirth? How do they come to know of these weddings? Why do they just show up without being invited? Are they just extortionists? And why do they not take singing lessons? (Pause.) Is it true? Could it be true what my mother used to say about them? Did they really put a curse on her because they did not allow them to sing and dance at their wedding? Or was that their explanation for not being able to have children of their own? Or...a reason to give to people for wanting to adopt me? (*CP* 16-17)

At long last she finds out the truth. The play ends with bathos as Uma reflects on that incident:

> They knew. Anarkali, Champa and all the hijra people knew who was behind the killing of Kamla. They have no voice. The case was hushed up and was not even reported in the newspapers. Champa was right. The police made no arrests. Subbu's suicide was written off as an accident. The photograph was destroyed. So were the lives of two young people. (*CP* 42)

This can be interpreted as a protest play against the injustice meted out to the downtrodden in a society. Dattani is questioning the age old belief of marriage being based on heterosexual relationship. He seems to say that homosexual and lesbian relationships being as natural as heterosexual relationship, same-sex marriage should be permitted in India. Laws should be made to this effect. Secondly, the plight of hijras in our society is deplorable. It is an irony of life that the hijras who are welcome on two occasions—one, at the time of marriage, and two at the time of childbirth—to sing and dance, are themselves deprived of marriage and childbirth. Nothing can be more ironical and pathetic than this. Dattani has done a good job by introducing a new theme to Indian English drama.

On a Muggy Night in Mumbai, the second play in Dattani's *Collected Plays* (2000), deals with gay personalities. The play begins with a conversation between Kamlesh and the guard in Hindi. Dattani without translating their conversation into English, takes recourse to transliteration. Kamlesh orders refreshments for his friends and asks the guards to make necessary arrangements. Later on Ed and Kiran came and began to chat. Since they are engaged, Ed assures his fiance with soothing words, 'Relax, I can take care of you'. Then came Sharad. He began to chat with Kamlesh. They have homosexual relationship. Again Kamlesh had homosexual relationship with Prakash, who is none other than Ed.

Since same-sex lane is unusal in Indian context, one can't help asking searching questions. One, is this play a true reflection of human behaviour in terms of same-sex relationship? Two, can 'gay themes of love' be a fit subject of contemporary drama? Dattani in course of his introduction to *Collected Plays* (2000) claims that his plays are the true reflection of the contemporary society. He opines that same-sex love is as natural as hetero-sexual love.

This view finds support in the following observations of John McRae with reference to the play, *On a Muggy Night in Mumbai.*

> And the themes of *On a Muggy Night* deserve to touch the whole of society and to be touched by it. It is not simply the first play in Indian theatre to handle openly gay themes of love, partnership, trust and betrayal. It is a play about how society creates patterns of behaviour and how easy it is for individuals to fall victim to the expectations society creates. (*CP* 45)

Characters like Sharad, Deepak, Kamlesh, Ed and Bunny are all gay personalities. Kamlesh has homosexual relationship with Sharad and Ed (Prakash) who is betrothed to his sister Kiran. In the end the truth is revealed and Ed and Kiran's engagement broke off. Each character in the play finally goes in search of his/her own identity and seeks to know what he/she has achieved or failed to achieve in life. Finally, Sharad speaking for himself, in a way sums up the feelings of all the characters in the following words:

I ask myself what I have got
And what I am and what I'm not.... (*CP* 111)

In this play, Dattani examines the psychology of persons who are by nature 'gays' or 'bi-sexuals' and the desire on the part of some of them to turn heterosexual. This is an unusual theme in the Indian context. But in real life such characters do exist. Hence, Dattani has re-created the characters in their own situations. The question that puzzles the mind is "What Makes A Man A Man" (*CP* 111).

Like the hijras, the gay and lesbian personalities suffer from exclusion in the Indian context. They are looked down upon by the society.

Do the Needful is built on the theme of 'gay' relationship and as a result the marital relationship is given a new twist to suit both the wife and the husband. This story though appears to be comical reminds us the abnormal behaviour of a young couple who are willing to pursue their pleasures independently outside marriage. Sally Avens has rightly analysed the play in "A Note on the Play" in the following words:

> In 1996 Mahesh Dattani was commissioned to write his first radio play for the BBC; the result was the somewhat unconventional 'romantic comedy', *Do the Needful.* Like all the best love stories, the hero and heroine end up getting married, but the road to marital bliss is full of the most unexpected twists and turns. For me, this was the joy of working on Mahcsh's script: his writing, whilst taking on a conventional form and being readily accessible to an audience, never fails to challenge and surprise. And whilst the play may be set in India within the conventions of 'arranged marriage', its wider themes are universal. A British audience found it easy to empathize with a gay man being forced to live his life within the norms of a heterosexual society or a young woman eager to prove her independence and break free from her parents. (*CP* 115)

Responding to a matrimonial advertisement, Mr. Chandrakant Patel and his wife come to Bangalore to see Lata Gowda, the daughter of Devraj Gowda and Prema Gowda for marriage to their son, Alpesh. The Gowdas are desperate to marry their daughter at the earliest. This is evident from their following conversations:

Prema Gowda.	Do you think it will work with these Patel people?
Devraj Gowda.	Who knows?
Prema Gowda.	They seem desperate.
Devraj Gowda.	We are desperate.
Prema Gowda.	He is thirty-plus and divorced.
Devraj Gowda.	She is twenty-four and notorious.

(*CP* 121)

Since it will be an inter-marriage the mother is apprehensive. And moreover, Alpesh is a divorcee. Devraj knows the nature of his daughter and therefore, wants her to get married—the sooner the better. The conversations between Patils and Gowdas reveal a good deal of things about the society in the present context.

Though Alpesh and Lata got married at the instance of their families, they never consummated their marriage. Lata is involved with a terrorist, Salim and Alpesh has homosexual relationship with Trilok. The title, "Do the Needful" is ironical in the context. That Alpesh and Lata managed to go in their own way notwithstanding their marriage, proves the point.

Ek Alag Mausam (*A Different Season*) is really a different kind of play on the latest dreaded disease HIV positive (AIDS). To write a play on AIDS victims and the reactions of the people to them is to bring alive the contemporary society which shows the predicament of human lives against the onslaught of this disease. Reader-Response criticism can be applied to this play to unfold human agony as well as selfishness of other people who avoid such diseased persons as untouchables. In this play a number of people are affected by this disease and Dattani shows how they live in the society knowing that their days are numbered. Aparna got the disease from her husband. Suresh and George got it through the transfusion of blood from his friend. Other patients got it from other sources like a child getting the virus from infected mother.

What is important in the play is the plight of the HIV positives on whose faces death stares each moment.... It is a death-in-life situation which needs human compassion to soothe and assuage their feelings.

The reaction of George's father is in a way the reaction of most of the people and their attitude to victims. George's father tells George harshly in his face to leave them. He says, "you may live for another seven years. But you have killed us before we have entered our graves.

What face do we have left in this village? (With great effort). Don't come back. Leave. Go George. (Making a gesture as if to a beggar) Go" (*CP* II 537).

Nothing can be more pathetic than this.

In the end, Dattani creates new situation in which Dr Machado makes an appeal to the public to change their attitude to HIV positives. The play ends with a hope that we may conquer AIDS as we have done other diseases in the past. "Today the world over doctors and scientists are trying to find a cure for Aids. In the interest of mankind we hope they succeed. While waiting for that cure to be invented or discovered, let us not forget—that miracles are known to happen" (*CP* II 556-57).

This is a heart touching play which shows human helplessness against the attack of the HIV positive virus. Let us try scientifically and pray for the success of the scientists. That is the message of the play.

Dattani's plays are about contemporary reality and therefore, the interaction between society and individual fascinates his imagination. Dattani makes it clear in his 'Preface' to *Collected Plays* (2000):

> I know that I am an artist. I don't need to underline it in my works. I write for my plays to be performed and appreciated by as wide a section of the society that my plays seek to and are about. (*CP* XI)

Dattani has the courage of conviction to write about unconventional themes such as love for hijras, gay and lesbian relationships and above all about stigmatized disease like Aids which cause social exclusion in the contemporary society. By portraying such victims as protagonists in his plays, Dattani calls for social inclusion for them. Though these plays are open to various kinds of interpretations, the two approaches which suit them most are Subaltern Studies and Queer theory. "Seven Steps Around the Fire" yields meanings when we apply the theory of Subaltern Studies to it. The hijras are subalterns, inferior in status in the society and they are incapable of raising their voices. They can't speak, they must be spoken for as Uma has done for them in "Seven Steps Around the Fire". They are 'marginals' in our society.

Dattani portrays sexuality as an important category of analysis of literary texts next to race, gender and class. Judith Butler, the author of *Bodies that Matter* (1993), questions fixed identities like heterosexuals, homosexuals and lesbians. All our identities come from differentiations from other identities. Paradoxically, identities are repetitions based on performances. It is in this sense that heterosexuality which takes itself as the only authentic form of sexuality, is 'a string of performances'. Heterosexuality sees itself as the authentic form of sexuality by relegating lesbianism and homosexuality to the background and discarding them as inauthentic. If heterosexuality is the center, other sexualities are the margins. Queer theorists now say that like gender, sexuality is a social construct. One can be either a heterosexual or homosexual and even both at the same time. What Dattani says is that it is homosexuality which causes to social exclusion. Hijras, homosexuals and Aids patients who suffer from social exclusion in our time, attract Dattani's attention. He portrays them sympathetically in his plays hoping for their inclusion into our society. There are hints and guesses in his plays which whispers results.

WORKS CITED

Avens, Sally. 'A Note on the Play', "Do the Needful", *Collected Plays,* Mahesh Dattani. New Delhi: Penguin Books, 2000.

Dattani, Mahesh. *Collected Plays.* New Delhi: Penguin Books, 2000.

———. *Collected Plays.* Vol. II. New Delhi: Penguin Books, 2005.

McRae, John. "A Note on the Play", "On a Muggy Night in Mumbai". Mahesh Dattani, *Collected Plays.* New Delhi: Penguin Books, 2000.

Critical Approaches to Mahesh Dattani's Plays

5

Literacy Criticism is an academic exercise. It is meant to explain, interpret, and evaluate literature for the benefit of those who read it (i.e. literature) for a course, an examination or to do research. For a general reader no such criticism is necessary. He reads literature for meaning, pleasure and enjoyment. That is why, for a general reader 'story' is most important and he reads that book—poetry, novel, story and even, a play—which reads like a story, has an appeal and may be, a quality of memorableness for him. This is precisely the reason for which a vast body of literature—stories, folk-tales, legends, etc.—exists in an oral form. It is handed down from generation to generation in the form of story-telling. Why, then do we need literary criticism? What is the purpose and outcome of it? Is it necessary to read literary criticism to understand and enjoy literature? The answer is and should be in the affirmative.

A literary text exists at several levels and has many layers of meanings. A general reader, by and large, is satisfied with the surface meaning of the text. Sometimes he also draws lessons from a text in terms of good and evil, reward and punishment to characters and upholds the morals of life. That is only a tip of the iceberg. The deep meaning of the text is unfolded before the readers by the literary critics who seek to interpret the text from several angles. Literary criticism not only facilitates the reading of a literary text but extends its meaning beyond the imagination of the author. Criticism makes a text important by extending its longevity beyond the lifetime of the writer. In a way, criticism is useful for the continuation or extension of the text from generation to generation. That is why, we have a number of schools of criticism and their bewildering varieties in the twentieth and twenty-first centuries which seek to explain the Author—Text—Reader—World quadrangle by measuring it from different angles.

What are the major schools of criticism prevalent in the West and in the English speaking world? In the twentieth century we have New Criticism, Russian Formalism, Myth Criticism, Archetypal Criticism, Structuralism, Deconstruction, Reader-Response Criticism, Feminist Criticism, Psychoanalytical Criticism, Marxist Criticism, Humanistic Criticism, New Historicism, Cultural Criticism, Postcolonial Criticism, Gender Studies and Queer Theory, as the outstanding schools of criticism that transcended the boundary of space and time. The question is which of the above schools of criticism is most suitable to analyse Dattani's plays. To my mind, Postcolonial Criticism, Gender Studies, Queer Theory and above all, Humanistic Criticism are most suitable to analyse and interpret Dattani's plays.

Gender Criticism, an off-shoot of Feminist criticism, takes the dichotomy between gender and sex seriously. For many critics, gender is a social and cultural construct, whereas sex is biological and natural. If the gender critics hold gender as a social and cultural construct, feminist critics take it (i.e. gender) as innate in terms of masculinity and feminity. This is brought out by Russ Murfin and Supriya M. Ray in the following passage:

> Certain gender critics have even questioned the distinction between heterosexuality and homosexuality, arguing that they, too, are social constructs. Many of these critics would also agree that sexuality as it is commonly perceived—as containing only two possibilities, homosexuality and heterosexuality—ignores the myriad variations and differences among individuals. Most people are not exclusively homo-or-hetero-sexual, these critics would argue. Such critics view sexuality as a continuum, not a fixed set of binary oppositions; they also recognize that sexuality

> encompasses a range of behaviours, from bondage to bestiality. Some gender critics (especially many gay and lesbian critics) also focus on sexuality but would disagree that it is culturally produced. These critics would argue that sexuality is innate, that homosexuals and heterosexuals are naturally different. (139)

Andrew Edgar and Peter Sedgwick have shown the difference between 'gender' and 'sex' in their book titled, *Key Concepts in Cultural Theory* in the following words:

> The concept of 'gender' is typically placed in opposition to the concept of 'sex'. While our sex (female/male) is a matter of biology, our gender (feminine/masculine) is a matter of culture. Gender may therefore be taken to refer to learned patterns of behaviour and action, as opposed to that which is biologically determined. Crucially, biology need not be assumed to determine gender. This is to suggest that while what makes a person male or female is universal and grounded in laws of nature, the precise ways in which women express their femininity and men express their masculinity will vary from culture to culture. Thus, qualities that are stereotypically attributed to women and men in contemporary western culture (such as greater emotional expression in women; greater tendencies to violence and aggression in men) are seen as gender, which entails that they could be changed. (158)

Keeping these approaches to 'gender' and 'sex' in mind let us take some of the plays of Dattani like *Seven Steps Around the Fire, On a Muggy Night in Mumbai, Do the Needful, Thirty Days is September and Mango Souffle* for a close study. *Seven Steps Around the Fire* is about hijras and same-sex love. To write a play on the lives of hijras seems not only to be unusual and unconventional but daring and revolutionary. Dattani has the courage of conviction to depict the lives of such people who are looked down upon by the society. The play begins with Uma Rao, a research scholar in Sociology trying to probe into the mystery of Kamla's (a hijra) death, by visiting Anarkali (another hijra) who is in jail on the charge of murdering the former. When Uma demands to knew about Kamla's death, Anarkali says:

> What is there to tell? I sing with other hijras at weddings and when a child is born. People give us money, otherwise I will put a curse on them (laughs). As if God is on our side (smokes), I did not do anything to Kamla. She was my sister (*CP* 12).

When Uma offered to take her on bail, Anarkali directed her to meet Champa, the head hijra at Russel Market in Shivajinagar. When Uma met Champa, the latter was both defiant and uncooperative. But gradually she gave in. She said:

> If I had the money I would throw it on that superintendent's face and get her back. Sons of whores, all of them...I know I said they would die in jail. But after all, I am the head hijra and she is my daughter. (*CP* 24)

From Champa, Uma got a clue on the basis of which she questioned Salim, the minister Mr Sharma's driver, it became clear that Salim used to visit Kamla regularly at the behest of Subbu, the minister's son. Later on a photograph was found showing the wedding between Kamla and Subbu. Anarkali revealed the truth in the end and Subbu killed himself on getting back his wedding photograph. This how she put it:

> Would you have believed me? Anyway, what is the use to all that? What does it matter who killed Kamla. She is dead.... So many times I warned her. First I thought Salim was taking by her for his own pleasure. When she told me about Subbu, madam, I tried to stop her. I fought with her. I scratched her face, hoping she will become ugly and Subbu will forget her. He wanted to marry her.... I was there at their wedding.... She gave me that picture to show to Champa. I saw the men coming for her. I told her to run.... (*CP* 41)

Uma unfolds the whole story before her husband in their bedroom:

> The photograph was what Mr. Sharma was after. A Polaroid picture that Subbu and Kamla had taken soon after their private wedding in some remote temple.... A picture of Kamla as a beautiful bride smiling at Subbu with the wedding garland around him. The Poojari probably didn't know that Kamla was not a woman. Of course, Mr. Sharma couldn't

> have it—totally unacceptable. So he arranged to have Kamla burned to death. But Salim had to tell him about the picture. Mr. Sharma simply had to have that picture. He sent Salim to threaten Anarkali and Champa.... He did get the picture eventually...after losing his son. What a price to pay! And now he will be arrested and tried for murder. (*CP* 41)

What Dattani highlights in the play is homosexual relationship and seems to ask why can't it be natural like heterosexual relationship and why can't there be marriage between homosexuals? The hijras are the subaltern. They can't speak for themselves. They must be spoken for. This is what Dattani does through the character of Uma, the researcher. The society looks down upon them after utilizing their services on the occasion of marriage and childbirth. Hence, gender studies and postcolonial criticism both apply to this play.

On a Muggy Night in Mumbai is again about same-sex love and homosexual relationship. Kamlesh, Ed (Prakash), Sharad, Bunny and Deepali all indulge in same-sex love. The whole play deals with unisexual and bisexual love relationship. Dattani examines this unusual love relationship among individuals both at psychological and physical level. He finds support from the Queer theorists on this unusual sexual relationship. If Eve Kosofsky Sedgwick examines the relationship between men (gay criticism) in literature and between gender and sexuality in *Between Men: English Literature and Male Homosocial Desire,* Judith Butler in her book, *Bodies that Matter* shows the relationships between gender and sexuality in the following paragraph:

> In Psychoanalytic terms, the relationship between gender and sexuality is in part negotiated through the question of the relationship between identification and desire. And here it becomes clear why refusing to draw lines of causal implication between these two domains is as important as keeping open an investigation of their complex interimplication. For, if to identify as a woman is not necessarily to desire a man, and if to desire a woman does not necessarily signal the constituting presence of a masculine identification, whatever that is, then the heterosexual matrix

> proves to be an 'imaginary' logic that insistently issues forth its own unmanageability. The heterosexual logic that requires that identification and desire to be mutually exclusive is one of the most reductive of heterosexiam's psychological instruments: if one identifies 'as' a given gender, one must desire a different gender. On the one hand, there is no one femininity with which to identify, which is to say that femininity might itself offer as array of identificatory sites, as the proliferation of lesbian feminine possibilities attests. On the other hand, it is hardly descriptive of the complex dynamic exchanges of lesbian and gay relationships to presume that homosexual identifications 'mirror' or replicate one another. The vocabulary for describing the difficult play, crossing, and destabilization of masculine and feminine identification within homosexuality has only begun to emerge within theoretical language: the non-academic language historically embedded in gay communities is here much more instructive. The thought of sexual difference 'within' homosexuality has yet to be theorized in its complexity. (Rice and Waugh 249)

Kamlesh is in love with Prakash (Ed), who is engaged to his sister Kiran. After Kiran's first marriage failed, she comes close to Ed and Ed intends to marry her. Deepali tells Kiran about it in the following words:

> He loves Ed, that is true. But he cared for you enough to tell you to marry Ed. Can't you see that? (*CP* 107)

At this Kiran gets angry and asks pointed questions to Ed.

> What did you want from me? What did you want from me so badly that you couldn't care how much you hurt me for it? (*CP* 107)

Having said this she gets nostalgic about her past and brings a comparison between Ed and her first husband. She says,

> When my husband beat me up. I truly believed and felt that he loved me enough to want to hurt me. Kamlesh helped me get out of that. But I continued being the same...woman, I wanted to feel loved by a man. In whichever way he wanted to love me. And I met you. And you did show love. And you

continue being the same...man.... If there any stereotypes around here, they are you and me'.... (*CP* 107)

Kamlesh and Ed had a photograph in compromising position which was found by the watchman. The neighbourhood came to know about it. Kamlesh had also homosexual relationship with Sharad and Kiran knew about it. Deepali seems to endorse this kind of relationship when she says, "I am all for the gay men's cause. Men deserve only men!" Needless to say that she herself is lesbian.

Bunny, a friend of Kamlesh, Ranjit and Sharad is a homosexual who is married. He tells Kiran, "I have never told anyone in so many words what I am telling you now—I am a gay man" (*CP* 103).

In the end all these friends in the end disperse when Sharad sings a song:

I ask myself what I have got
And what I am and what I'm not.... (*CP* 111)

The play is about 'gay' and 'lesbian' persons who pretend to be different in public. Dattani dives deep into the psyche of these types of persons who think they have a right to pursue their pleasure and live in their own way.

Behind their desire to seek same-sex love, there lies the agony of finding an identity of their own. That becomes the burden of the plays. Living in darkness away from the purview of an open society, these characters are torn between desire and recognition. They fail to fulfil their desire as it is crushed under the norms of the society and lose their identity as individuals. Their love remains unnatural and their identity is threatened in a society which only upholds heterosexual relationship leading to marriage.

The characters presented in the play are pleasure seekers. Their sexuality is threatened by the norms of the society. They want to throw away the traditional and conventional pattern of seeking love through heterosexual relationship. Their nature is different from that of normal social human beings. There is a binary opposition between their nature and the culture of their society. This dichotomy between nature and culture obstructs their love and poisons their minds. The note of revolt against the society is unmistakable. In the age of globalization, nature triumphs over culture.

Thirty Days in September shows sexual exploitation of young girls and women by men who are their blood relations. The norms of morality are thrown to the wind. Mala, a young woman was abused sexually by her maternal uncle in her childhood and later on she became free with young men like Deepak who proposed to marry her. Shanta, Mala's mother knew everything and was upset with her daughter. Mala bears a grudge against the male-dominated society and turns down Deepak's proposal of marriage. Thus, Deepak tells Shanta:

> I just don't get it, I thought everything was going well (Upset). I thought she loved me. May be I said or did something to upset her. But what could it be?... (Composing himself). Last week, I told her that she was the most intelligent, sensitive and dynamic woman I had met. She just stared at me and said, "I have something to tell you. It is over. I don't want to continue with our relationship." She doesn't want to see me ever again. (*CP* II 14)

Mala has a guilt consciousness—for being exploited sexually and also being an accomplice in her puberty and early youth—and that is why, she is indecisive about her action. This is how she puts it before her mother:

> I don't know why. I just don't understand.... Please don't ask me why I do it, it's just a game...not a game, ...I know it's wrong....I have no character ... I suppose it's these Western Values, I wish I were more traditional then I wouldn't behave like this.... It has to end in a month's time. In fact I like it best when I can time it so it lasts for thirty days. I even mark it on my calendar. After that, I have to—move on, if you know what I mean...well it means that it is no longer satisfying to me, and I don't mean the physical part of it, although that is usually the main attraction for me...not that I actually enjoy it when they are doing it to me...sometimes I do with the right kind of people...usually older men though not necessarily so. Deepak my fiance, is only a few years older to me.... I think I like it—I don't know how to put it....

> The only person who can, who could have prevented all this is my mother. Sometimes I wish she would just tell me to stop. She could have prevented a lot from happening. (*CP* II 18)

Mala's reaction comes out of her anger caused by her mother's inaction to protect her from her uncle. She in her teens is unable to resist her uncle's advances and gradually gives in. That kind of submission makes her disappointed. Out of disappointment in life she is driven to the arms of man. Mala danced with 'Man' and held him tight in a party in the presence of 'Man's' fiance, Radhika. She went to the extent of saying, "Do whatever you want with me, but take me with you now." Later on in the play it is revealed that both Mala and her mother Shanta were physically exploited by Mala's maternal uncle, 'The Man'. Both suffered psychologically and Shanta's husband left them. When Mala learnt from her mother that she was also exploited by the same man during her childhood, she understood the plight of the mother. In the end comes the heart to heart union between the mother and the daughter. This is how the play ends with Mala's words:

> It is not your fault mother. Just as it wasn't my fault. Please, tell me that you have forgiven me for blaming you.... I know you will, mother, I know you have. (*CP* II 58)

Apart from Queer theory this play, *Thirty Days in September* can be interpreted in terms of Feminist criticism which shows the exploitation of women by men. In a patriarchal society women become toys at the hands of men. It is social and cultural construct of feminine mind which fights shy of going against men. We can also apply psychoanalytical criticism to this play. The subconscious mind of Mala holds her mother responsible for the torture meted out to her. She asks her mother:

> Where were you when he (her uncle) locked the door to your bedroom while I was napping in there? Where were you during those fifteen minutes when he was destroying my soul? Fifteen minutes everyday of my summer holidays, add them-up. Fifteen minutes multiplied by thirty or thirty-one or whatever. That's how long or how little it took for you to send me to hell for the rest of my life! (*CP* II 53)

Shanta is full of remorse when she recalls the physical exploitation in the past and the subconscious mind makes her feel guilty about it. She confesses before her daughter in the following words:

> I was six, Mala, I was six. And he (her brother) was thirteen...and it wasn't only summer holidays. For ten years!... (pointing to the picture of God) I looked to Him.... He helped me. By taking away all feeling. No pain, no pleasure, only silence. Silence means Shanti. Shanti...I cannot even speak about it. (*CP* II 55)

Dattani brings the theme of incest into this play and shows another angle of human life in which the dichotomy between appearance and reality is so glaring.

Apart from writing about the physical aspect of human life in terms of human passion for all kinds of love and lust, Dattani has chosen beautiful themes like human compassion and contemporary reality for some of his plays. *Final Solutions, Clearing the Rubbles* and *A Tale of a Mother Feeding Her Child* deal with themes of contemporary life and reality. In his well-known play, *Final Solutions,* Dattani depicts the communal tensions and riots with insight and objectivity. Daksha (Hardika) the grandmother reads her diary to reinforce her feelings about the jubilations over the country getting independence in August 1947 and regrets the communal riots which followed immediately. She reads from her diary:

> We... (tries hard to read her handwriting) ...gained independence. You should have seen it. Everyone was awake waiting for midnight—like children on the last day of school, waiting for the last bell of the last class before vacation. And their rushing out and screaming and shouting and fighting. (*CP* 116)

Immediately after that a procession passed through the lanes and the chorus followed:

> Chorus 2, 3. They broke our rath
>
> They broke our Chariot and felled our God! (*CP* 168)

The curfew was clamped and the 'Muslim girls' hostel was bombed'. Smita, the granddaughter of Hardika was worried about her friend, Tasneem who was inside the hostel. Smita and her father Ramnik contacted Tasneem's father, Mr. Noor Ahmed on phone and told him to come to Amargaon to take his daughter. In the meanwhile the chorus grew louder and two persons Bobby and Javed entered Ramnik's house who gave him protection against the wishes of his wife, Aruna and mother, Hardika. Ramnik boldly faced the mob and refused to hand over Bobby and Javed to them. Smita knew both Bobby and Javed. She supported her father's stand to let them stay for the night. When the father insisted on knowing them, she said:

> This is Tasneem's brother, Javed and this...is Babban—Bobby—Tasneem's fiance. (*CP* 189)

What she did not tell was that she was in love with Bobby in the college.

The deep-rooted misunderstanding between two communities—the Hindus and the Muslims—was brought out by the conversations and arguments between Ramnik and Javed. Ramnik thought that Muslims were violent and Javed argued that they were provoked by Hindus to be so. These are matters of opinion and debate devoid of reason.

Bobby tells later on in the play that Javed was humiliated by a Hindu neighbour who wiped the place where he had placed his (i.e. the neighbour's) letter and wiped the letter before picking it up. Some people flare up communal tension and see the fun of people doing violence against each other. The police is not serious to quell the communal riots and instead, pretends not to have seen anything. When Ramnik threatens Javed to hand over him to the police, Javed ridicules it.

> Javed. Arrest me? When they have been looking the other way all along. How do you think we got into the street? In their vans. They will arrest me. Don't worry. To please people like you. And a few innocent Muslims to please every one. (*CP* 204)

Javed also admits that he is like the mob which made an attack on him. He sardonically comments:

> Ha! You want to throw me to the mob? I am a part of it. You have been protecting me from people like me. I'm no different from them.... I do what they are doing—only on a different street! (*CP* 204)

Javed admitted that he was with the mob when the chariot came. He went to the priest but did not kill him. He regretted to have been there.

Unlike Javed, Bobby was broad-minded like Ramnik and Smita. But Aruna was not. Aruna would not like Javed or Bobby to touch the small brasspot which is meant for carrying pooja water. When Smita objects to it, Aruna retorts.

What kind of sanskar will you give them (i.e., Smita's children when she gets married) when you don't have any yourself? It is all very well to have progressive ideas. But are you progressing or are you drifting? God knows, I don't want all this violence.... For many generations we have preserved our Sanskar because we believe it is the truth!... And I will not have it all perish to accommodate someone else's faith. (*CP* 210)

Bobby comes to the Puja room and holds the image of Lord Krishna in his hand. He tells loudly:

> He does not burn me to ashes? He does not cry out from the heaven's saying He has been contaminated!... Look how He rests in my hands! He knows I cannot harm Him. He knows his strength! I don't believe in Him but He believes in me. He smiles! He smiles at our trivial pride and our trivial shame. (*CP* 224)

Smita does not believe in fasting and praying. She has no prejudice against anyone. Ramnik wants to give job to Javed in his shop because that shop originally belonged to a Muslim which was burnt in a communal riot. Ramnik wants to make amends. Hardika after hearing her son regrets the past.

This is a play on communal hatred based on age-old suspicion and mistrust. If people became liberal-minded like Ramnik, Bobby and Smita and see reason, the evil of communal hatred will be wiped out from the minds of the people. All religion in the end is one and the same religion—that is faith in God, in whatever form He may be worshipped. Dattani not only suggests but through his characters 'whispers results'.

How love can transform a person and make her compassionate is shown in the character of Anna Gosweb in *The Tale of a Mother Feeding Her Child* (a radio play). A foreign woman Anna comes to India (i.e. Gujarat) to see the man she met and fell in love with years ago. Finding the man dead and seeing his family (wife and children) in distress, she helps ungrudgingly. Anna describes her feelings on seeing Jaman's wife in the following words:

> I was her late husband's girlfriend. Nobody can be mature about such things. I didn't have words to tell her that it was just one of those one night things. I wanted to tell her that he slept with me only for the money, probably to buy her a new sari or something. That's why he travelled all the way to Goa, right? To earn some money to bring back to his family, I got a great deal more out of it. More than I wanted really. I—I was only nineteen! Of course! I am glad I have Jennifer...such a lovely girl. (*CP* II 568)

She takes the child, Shanti, Jaman's daughter to the town against all odds and gives her medical treatment and finally saves her life.

When one is in true love with another, nationality, colour and social status don't matter. Love transcends all—Dattani seems to say. These two plays (*Final Solutions* and *The Tale of Mother Feeding Her Child*) can be interpreted best in terms of Humanistic Criticism. M.H. Abrams in course of an article titled, "What is a Humanistic Criticism?" says that, "a humanistic literary criticism is one that deals with a work of literature as composed by a human being, for human beings, and about human beings and matters of human concern." (JLC 8:2 21) These two plays are about human beings who are greatly affected by communal riots and poverty respectively, which cause greater concern for mankind.

Dattani has dealt with crime as a theme in two of his well-known plays titled *Uma and the Fairy Queen* and *The Swami and Winston.* Dattani unravels the mystery of Michael's murder at the hands of his wife Nila in *Uma and the Fairy Queen.* Nila Ahmed, a T.V. star from Pakistan married Michael after divorcing her first husband Mr Malik. Her son, Feroz was financially helped by Michael who sponsored his education. But when Michael refused to divorce Nila, she planned his murder and finally killed him. There is a hint in the play that she had an affair with Mr Liam Tate, the British Cultural Ambassador to India. Mr Liam told Uma, a detective and police officer Suresh's wife about the strained relationship between Nila and Michael: "Their marriage is falling apart, it's an open secret in London, but it's not something they like to talk about." When Uma asked Feroz, Nila's son, "why do you think she (Nila) would kill her husband?" he said, "Because she is in love with this whiteman!" (Liam) and added that he saw them together, "Everywhere! In the hotel! In his room! She is a whore! Michael died because of her" (*CP* II 457).

This play exposes the vulgar display of the lust of a woman leading to her criminal action resulting in the death of her second husband. Feroz, her son exposes his mother before Liam and Uma in the following words:

> Feroz. Well, you two wanted to know the truth.... She was a famous T.V. Star.... She thought she could do whatever she wanted to do.... She was an immoral woman and that is something we don't forgive. She slept with her actor friends! For money, for pleasure or just to please the Devil. And I was born out of her cesspool of lust. (To Nila) You! You don't know what I had to suffer. In school I was known as the bastard! At home I was the unwanted child. We had to move to India and live in hiding to run away from the disgrace, but you won't let us live in peace. (*CP* II 465)

This play can also be read as a play of protest against the perpetuation of colonial culture. The British Council's decision to bring a Shakespeare Company to mark the Indian Independence Day was criticized by Suresh, the Superintendent of Police. He tells about it to his wife, Uma in the following words:

> Bringing a Shakespeare company to mark out Independence Day! If you ask me, they only want to remind us that they ruled over us. (*CP* II 428)

The Swami and Winston is a play about pseudo-religious people who cheat others in the name of religion by wearing masks. It is a veiled criticism of the religious fundamentalists who exploit the people and manage to escape from the clutches of law. Researcher, Uma, the wife of Superintendent of Police, Suresh and daughter-in-law of Deputy Commissioner, with help of the constable, Munswamy unravels the mystery of the murder of Lady Montefiore.

Lady Montefiore came to India to meet her brother Charles Montefiore who was staying in an Ashram in Whitefield with the Swamiji. This is how Charles reacts to his sister's killing.

> My sister...my sole relative...'sole' as in 'only'...came to India to visit me. She wanted me to go back to England with her. She loved me and she thought she knew what was good for me.... I tried to explain to her that I was a deeply unhappy person in England. I didn't know it then.... I know it after Swamiji's blessings...here in this ashram I have found happiness. I have never experienced before. I feel sad that someone got something out of killing my sister...I do miss her terribly, but India and Swamiji have taught me how to deal with this loss. (*CP* II 312)

Charles came to India after meeting an Indian in London who spoke on Advaita philosophy and that person turned out 'to be the most bigoted, racist, carteist, classist man' for him. Though the suspicion about Lady Montefiore's murder first fell on her brother and later on the Swamiji, Sitaram Trivedi, the Pseudo-Advaita Philosophy scholar turned out to be the person behind her murder. The five-thousand pound cheque which Lady Montefiore issued to Mr Sitaram Trivedi for finding out her dog, Winston, finally was given to constable Munswamy who looked after the dog.

Dattani here exposes those pseudo-religious persons who play dirty politics in the name of religion. This is a biting satire on persons indulging in criminal acts under the façade of religious activities in contemporary society in India.

Dance Like a Man is the masterpiece of Dattani in which he shows two attitudes to it. The old conservative attitude to 'Dance' as a profession is not very respectable but new attitude to it is both progressive and honourable. Ratna, the protagonist, a noted dancer is very happy with Jairaj, a dancer and an admirer of the art. This couple has perfect understanding as they continue to perform on stage year after year. Amritlal, Jairaj's father is dead against 'dance' as a profession and would not like his daughter-in-law to go to a prostitute to learn the art of dancing and his son to grow long hairs. Lata, daughter of Ratna and Amritlal, is also a dancer and her mother moved heaven and earth to give her scope to earn a name for herself. Ratna loves, practices and worships the art and learns sitting at the feet of Chennai Amma: "To master the art of abhinava, you will have to find the woman and God inside you—and to dance, you must fight the demons outside you" (*CP* II 118).

But 'dance' as an 'art' has its pitfalls and social repercussions. It breeds jealousy, suspicion and brings misunderstanding in the family—more so, if both the husband and wife are dancers. For example, when Lata got applause and standing ovation from the Chief Minister and Ratna took all the credit for it, Jairaj became jealous. This is how Dattani expresses the sentiments of the wife and husband in the following lines:

Ratna. You are too kind. Sathyu Sahid being such a senior government official, you are also so knowledgeable about dance...if people like you praise her, she has every reason to be thrilled.

Jairaj exchanges a look with Vishwas.

And the Chief Minister himself gave her a standing ovation.

Did you see? As soon as Lata finished her tillance, he stood up and applauded.

Jairaj (to Viswas). He was in a hurry to go to the toilet. (*CP* II 142)

This betrays Jairaj's sense of distancing himself from the encouragement which his wife, Ratna gives to their daughter. Unwittingly Jairaj echos his father, Amritlal in disapproving the attitude of the next generation towards dance. But Ratna is determined to make her an accomplished dancer and works in that direction.

Earlier in the play Ratna requested Chandrakala, a fellow dancer, to lend Seshadri, a flutist for her daughter's show, and she reluctantly agreed, Ratna made a disparaging comment on her. This is how the conversation between Jairaj and Ratna goes:

Jairaj. What do you mean he will only give us a day's rehearsal? He can't be rehearsing with Chandrakala all the day for the rest of the days.

Ratna. When he's not rehearsing with her, he's sleeping with her.

Jairaj. That's just gossip.

Ratna. It's not gossip. I've seen it with my own eyes.

Jairaj. When?

Ratna. When we were in Moscow, at the hotel. At three in the morning. I saw him sneak down the corridor and into her room. (*CP* II 127)

Later on in the play, Amritlal played a trick on Ratna by permitting her to dance and stopping Jairaj from dancing. He struck a deal with Ratna and implored upon her to make him 'a man'. As time rolled on, the wife and the husband drifted apart and became victims of professional jealousy. This is how Dattani brings the differences between the wife and the husband to light:

Jairaj. Whose fault is that only you get invitation to dance?

Ratna. Not mine.

Jairaj. For one whole year I didn't dance—turning down offers because I didn't want to dance alone.

Ratna. I didn't ask for such a sacrifice. Tell me what you want. I'll do anything.

Jairaj. I want you to give me back...give me back my self-esteem.

Ratna. When did I ever take it?

Jairaj. Bit by bit. Insisting on top billing in all our programmes. Making me dance my weakest items. Focusing the entire... Show....

Ratna. Face it, Jairaj. It's me they want to see dancing. (*CP* II 160-61)

It is here that 'the wheel has turned a full circle' and the wife and husband have drifted apart forever. Professional jealousy breaks off all relationship—be it between friends, or couples. When one runs after fame and fortune, love takes a back seat. No wonder, wife and husband become rivals and the 'green eyed monster' (i.e. jealousy) eats up marital bond. Ratna and Jairaj are classic examples of the victims of professional jealousy and rivalry.

Morning Raga, a play about Carnatic music and musicians, can be interpreted from psycho-analytical point of view. The inner urge of an artist and a musician is to reach out to the audience. However, a musician or an artist does not make her intention explicit. The protagonist, Swarnalatha who lost her friend Vaishnavi in a bus accident became indifferent to her art. Abhinay, Vaishnavi's son had music in his blood, compelled Swarnalatha to come out of her self-imposed reticence to perform in a town. Abhinay was supported by Priyanka (Pinkie) and her mother, Mrs Kapoor to practice music by forming a music group. But Abhinay's father was opposed to it.

Abhinay came to Swarnalatha's house to persuade her to sing for his musical group. A reluctant Swarnalatha asked Abhinay with which raga he would like to start. Abhinay, on the other hand asked her in which raga she would prefer to sing. Swarnalatha said that, "you must always start with a Ganesh Shotram. He is the God that will remove all your obstacles. (To Abhinay) Can you play in raga Todi?" With this, her inner urge to sing and teach singing to others began to surface.

Abhinay tries his best to make Swarnalatha overcome her shyness to perform in a concert in the city. By bringing his mother's violin with him, he tries to win over her emotionally. This is how the conversation goes:

Abhinay. Will you sing for me in a concert?

Swarnalatha. No.

Abhinay. You must. I cannot do the concert without you.

Swarnalatha. Why?

Abhinay. I don't know. It somehow makes sense.

Swarnalatha. I don't go to the city.

Abhinay. You must.

Swarnalatha. Why?

Abhinay. Because it's me who is asking. Vaishnavi's son. My mother played for you. You can sing for me. Or don't you want to return the favour because she is dead and it does not matter any more?

Abhinay storms out leaving a disturbed Swarnalatha. Mr. Shastri appears.

Swarnalatha. He wants me to sing in a concert.

Mr Shastri. Do it! Do it and get it over with. (*CP* II 380-81)

Apart from her desire to perform Carnatic music, Swarnalatha has a guilt consciousness to overcome. That is, she makes herself responsible for Vaishnavi's death. That is why, she performs ritual for her dead friend and after that she gains courage to practice music. She tells Abhinay's father, who is dead against his son's musical group, boldly that she will teach him music and make him worthy of his late mother: "I can teach him raga. I can teach him tala. Let us see whether he has inherited some bhava from his mother."

Abhinay's father is opposed to his son's venture of building a musical group by taking a loan. The dichotomy between the father and the son is brought out in the following words:

Abhinay. Ya.... This is about a loan.... No, it's not a housing loan.... It's for a concert...ya, you heard right...well, a music concert... stop laughing.... Oh, you are coughing, I am sorry I thought you were.... Wait. I can offer a collateral...my apartment.... Fine I will come over with the papers—tomorrow?... What time?... Sure. Thanks.

His father overhears this conversation.

Abhinay's father. Do you think you will back all that money? From a music concert?

Abhinay. Yes. It will come back to me.

Abhinay's father. And if it doesn't?

Abhinay. I will. I know....

Abhinay's father. If it doesn't come back, you will return to my home and fulfil your duties as a son.

Abhinay. I am so sure it will, I can even agree to those terms.

Abhinay heads towards his room. He turns around to face his father.

You must have said that to my mother too...fulfil your duties. But I am certain my mother didn't question you about your role as a husband or father. Neither will I.

He goes in.

Abhinay's father. I brought you up! Not your mother! She never cared for you, she never cared for me! I knew on my wedding night that she didn't love me! She only cared for that woman and her music! (*CP* II 397)

We can apply Marxist criticism to this play if we take Abhinay's father's attitude to music vis-à-vis loss and gain in terms of economic considerations. If life is to be measured in terms of profit and loss, then music has no place in practical life. Abhinay's father warns him: "You are going to lose all your money and she is not going to help you when you go knocking on her door".

Swarnalatha tells Abhinay's father boldly that "they are laughing at your son today. Tomorrow they will salute him for his talents. But then he will be Vaishnavi's son."

When argument fails, love triumphs. Swarnalatha was won over by the affection and love of Abhinay and Pinkie. In her living room Swarnalatha teaches Pinkie, Sindu Bhairavi, a raga that Vaishnavi specialized by playing on the latter's violin. When Pinkie asks, "What?", Swarnalatha says:

> That is the name of the raga I am going to teach now. It's a morning raga. It's—very special to me. It was Vaishnavi's favourite raga. It was the raga I was planning to sing....

While Swarnalatha was playing, Abhinay came in. He was pleasantly surprised.

> "That's it! That's the raga I want. That's what I was looking for, don't you see! (To Pinkie) My mother never played that for me! She only played it for her."

The guilt in the subconscious mind of Swarnalatha made her nervous in all those twenty years since the bus accident in which her son and friend, Vaishnavi died. When that mystery was unravelled by Pinkie, Swarnalatha regained her strength and was cured of her bad conscience. It was Pinkie's father who was driving the car which dashed against the bus causing the accident. Pinkie asked Abhinay and Swarnalatha to sit in her car and she drove the car over the bridge to clear the mystery of that accident. This is how the play goes:

> Pinkie. I hope you will find it in you to forgive me.
>
> *Pinkie puts her car in top gear and speeds towards the bridge.*
>
> *Swarnalatha realizes that she is going over the bridge. Her panic attack starts.*
>
> Swarnalatha. No! Please! Stop the car!
>
> Pinkie. I just went to show you that it is not your fault!
>
> Abhinay. What are you doing?
>
> Pinkie. To show you that there is no curse on you!
>
> *Swarnalatha holds on to Pinkie to prevent her from driving further.*
>
> Swarnalatha. Stop it! Stop the car! We will all die.
>
> Abhinay (*holding Swarnalatha back*). Calm down! Stop the car! *Swarnalatha*

looks outside and sees the bridge approaching. A truck passed by in full speed.

Swarnalatha (*gasping for breath*). No!

Swarnalatha watches in horror as they cross the bridge. Her head spins. The car reaches the other side of the bridge and Pinkie pulls over. Abhinay opens the door for Swarnalatha. Swarnalatha rushes out gasping for air. She runs to a tree and sits down, not looking at the bridge. Pinkie follows her.

Pinkie. You see. Nothing happened. It is not a curse on you! I knew that nothing would happen, because you are not to blame. Look at me please.... Pinkie holds Swarnalatha so that they are looking into each other's eyes. Abhinay joins them on the edge. 'It was my father'.... He was driving the car.

Swarnalatha is still dazed but is listening to Pinkie now. Abhinay stands still at this revelation.

He...my father...was a very unhappy man. I was too small then to know that. I thought he was happy. He loved me. He really loved me. I know that. But he was unhappy...and he took to drink... (*Pleading now.*) I know that if he were alive he would beg for your forgiveness.... Please try to forgive him.... He made a big mistake. He shouldn't have been driving but...he did.... If you cannot forgive him, at least don't blame yourself for what happened....

Pinkie looks on at Swarnalatha, waiting for a response. Swarnalatha slowly stands up and walks towards the bridge. She sees the bridge in a new light. She talks in a deep breath. Pinkie comes closer to her awaiting forgiveness. She bugs Pinkie. Swarnalatha breaks away from Pinkie and goes to Abhinay.

Swarnalatha. It doesn't matter whose fault it was. The truth is that your mother is gone and so is my son. Can any force bring them back to us? Can any force bring back her father? No. (*CP* II 409-10)

This is the turning point Swarnalatha's life. She has a clear conscience now. She moves from pessimism to optimism. She gets a new lease of life. Hence, the confidence.

Swarnalatha. So, go to the city and don't think about these things. Go. (To Pinkie) You have my blessings, if that is what you want. (*CP* II 411).

Abhinay's letter to Swarnalatha casts a magic spell over her. Her love for Abhinay conquers her fear of the past sad incident. Mr. Shastri, Swarnalatha's husband reads the letter as follows:

> You are wrong. There are forces that can bring back your son and my mother to us. I hope one day I can help you understand how proud your son would be if you sang for him. I don't know how to make you see that, but I will keep trying. (*CP* II 411-12)

Swarnalatha goes to the city in response to this letter and performs the raga. The end turns out to be happy as Swarnalatha and Abhinay are united in love as a mother and a son. Music bridges the gap and heals human heart by filling it with love. That's the unique conclusion of this play. Dattani could not have done better. Here is the healing touch.

Swarnalatha. Thank you. It has been difficult raga for me to learn. Twenty years is a long time. Music is a never ending journey. It has been my dream to sing for an audience such as you. But...tonight, I will sing this song for my son who, like my music, has returned after a very long journey. Abhinay, I sing this raga for you—my son. (*CP* II 416)

In *Do the Needful* the protagonists, Alpesh Patel and Lata Gowda who come from different family backgrounds get married through negotiations between two families. But their marital bliss eludes them as their minds are pre-occupied with the thoughts of other people with whom they are in love. Lata thinks of Salim, a terrorist with whom she is in love and Alpesh being a gay thinks of Trilok with whom he has homosexual relationship. The play which begins with a note of negotiation between Patel and Gowda families, ends with the protagonists choosing to live their lives in their own way behind the façade of marriage.

What is important in the play is not the love or hate between the protagonists but the depiction of contemporary reality in terms of north-south divide and the hiatus between the rich and the poor and above all dowry given in marriages. The common people protest against the marriage between the South Indian and North/West Indians. This is how the coconut vendor reacts to Lata and Alpesh marriage:

> Those sons of demons! Who asked them to come here? (*Shouts after the car.*) Go away! We don't want your money! Go! (*Spitting loudly in anger.*) I am a son of this soil, this is my land! We don't want you, you sons of whores! Born in the most inauspicious time! (*To Devraj Gowda*). And you! You we have served for so long, you give your daughters to them. Aiyo! Big people! Modern people! (*Fades out as he walks away with his cycle.*) Kaliyuga! Kaliyuga! (*CP* 141)

But Kusumben Patel, Alpesh's mother under constraint agrees to accept her daughter-in-law from the Gowda family. She says, "they are South Indian but now-a-days all that is changing.... It is not a question of what I like or don't like. We are begging, what is the point in hiding the begging bowl?"

How industry is consuming all the electricity leaving the villages high and dry is brought out by the conversation between Devraj Gowda (Lata's father) and Alpesh in the following lines:

> Devraj Gowda. It is all because of those blood illegal industrialists! They don't even spare our halli! Siphoning the electricity from the poles! All crooks, I tell you! All, all of

them are thieves! They should be thrown out of the state. Let them do all this in their own state.

Pause Alpesh (quietly). Not all industrialists are thieves—sir.

Devraj Gowda. I know. It is all those corrupt government officers who are encouraging all this just to line their pockets. Rotten to the core! Our country has gone to the dogs because of them. (*CP* 144-45)

Again Dattani brings the caste and region factors as obstacles to marriage in India to the notice of the readers and audience through the conversation between Chandrakant Patel and Devraj Gowda. This how he puts it:

Chandrakant Patel. But you can still consider a proposal from us for your daughter. I understand there will be reasons for not seeking a groom in your own community. We are also in a...similar situation. But it must be so difficult for you....

Pause.

Devraj Gowda. Who can stop change.... I...I...don't know what to say. I know my parents and my forefathers will be hurt very badly, and I am...betraying them, but...my daughter's happiness is most important. Please. Sir, please accept my daughter. (*CP* 147)

Finally, Dattani exposes Alpesh, who is a homosexual, getting involved with Mali, who treats Lata as his elder sister. Lata gets furious with Alpesh and decides to run away. She angrily says,

> You filthy beast! How could you force him to do all that?... Mariappa and his smuggler friends will be passing by now. I will take a ride with them to wherever the sandalwood is going.... My Salim lives in Bombay. (*CP* 153-55)

This play is about social problems and contemporary changing society in which old prejudices as well as values are making way for new adjustments. Above all, it shows the liberated young men and women who pursue their sexual pleasures in unconventional ways.

The breaking up of joint-family system in India is on the rise now. Dattani takes it as a theme in some of his plays like, *Where There's Will* and *Bravely Fought the Queen* in the same way as A.K. Ramanujan does in his family-poems. In *Where There's a Will* Dattani gives a twist to family disharmony by bringing the wife and the mistress together. It is an irony of fate that the woman who keeps the family together is not the wife but the mistress.

Hasmukh Mehta, the patriarch of the family wants his son, Ajit to follow his line as he did by emulating his father, which the son resents. Again he wants his wife, Sonal to be active and smart in life. Having failed in both the counts he keeps a mistress Kiran and makes a Will making her the custodian of his property. This play can be best interpreted in terms of psycho-analytic criticism and humanistic criticism. Let us take two of Hasmukh Mehta's dialogues why he did so.

Hasmukh. My father had only me to help him out. He took great trouble to make sure I didn't turn out like my brother. No more school. No more loafing for me. Hard work. And I am happy he did that! We made money! I remember we used to spend half the night going through our accounts and counting our profits. The other half of the night we would dream of being millionaires! (*Puffs on the cigarette again.*) Then when I was twenty-one, the greatest tragedy of my life took place. I got married to my wife. Sonal. You will soon meet her. The following year Ajit was born. Tragedy after tragedy. Still, they proved lucky, I suppose. Within no time we were running a very successful export house. Mehta Exports. And then another—Ajit exports. My wife insisted I name it after him. Today, I, Hasmukh Mehta, am one of the richest men in this city. All by my own efforts. Forty-five

> years old and I am a success in capital letters. Twenty-three years old and he is on the road to failure, in bold capital letters! At his age, I was a mature responsible man, not eating my father's head and nibbling at papads! (*CP* 464)

If this is his opinion about his son, the worse is about his wife. This is how Hasmukh puts it:

> Sonal. My wife. My son's mother. Do you know what Sonal means? No? 'Gold'. When we were newly married. I used to joke with her and say she was as good as gold. But that was when we were newly married. I soon found out what a good-for-nothing she was. As good as mud. Ditto our sex life. Mud. Twenty-five-years of marriage and I don't think she has ever enjoyed sex. Twenty-five years of marriage and I haven't enjoyed sex with her. So what does a man do? You tell me. I started eating out. Well, I had the money. I could afford to eat in fancy places. And what about my sex life? Well, I could afford that too. Those expensive ladies of the night in five star hotels! (*Smiles at some pleasant memories.*) Some of them were really...! But that didn't go on for long. I mean, a man in my position has to be careful. I needed a safer relationship. Something between a wife and a pick-up. Yes. A mistress! It didn't take me very long to find her. She was right there in my office. An unmarried lady. Not an ordinary typist or even a secretary. A shrewd hard-headed marketing executive. If there was anyone in my office who had brains to match mind, it was her. She is now one of the directors of the company. Not entirely due to her shrewd head. She lives now in a company flat in a posh locality. I won't tell you where. Well, it's walking distance from here. Convenient for me. All right, what's wrong with having a bit on the side? Especially since the main course is always without salt. Okay, okay, less salt. (*CP* 473)

Ajit and his wife, Preeti on their part, disliked Hasmukh. Ajit didn't like to follow his father's footprints and his wife Preeti, who married only for money is disappointed. About Hasmukh's Will she says,

> The whole world is saying, 'Hasmukh Mehta didn't have faith in his own family. He didn't get along with his wife. His son is a spend-thrift. His daughter-in-law is a scheming little witch. That's why he left all his wealth in the hands of an outsider.' We've got to show them that he was...influenced. By this woman. (*CP* 493)

Kiran sought back:

> I think I must clear some misunderstandings you may have about my authority. I am only the trustee of all his wealth. Not the owner. I get a fixed salary for my job. Everything rightfully belongs to the three of you. Provided you follow his instructions. Ajit will have to attend office as usual. He will get a detailed brief on his duties tomorrow. Mrs Mehta, you shall get a regular allowance to run the house, and a little more for your personal expenses. And Preeti, you too will get an allowance—when you become a mother. When your child is twenty-one, the trust automatically dissolves. Its holdings will be transferred to Ajit for him and his heirs to enjoy. (*CP* 493)

In the end Sonal understood her mistake and Kiran forgave Preeti for her treachery of exchanging Hasmukh's Blood Pressure medicine with her Vitamins and the whole family came together. What Hasmukh could not do, Kiran did with her patience and understanding. Emotional attachments are far more stronger than intellectual snobbishness in keeping the family together. It is not the head but the heart that rules in family-matters and human relationship. The message is loud and clear.

Bravely Fought the Queen shows how women suffer at the hands of their husbands in the joint family. Moreover, the homosexual husbands enact hell for their wives. This play in three acts shows men and women in opposition to each other. The result is disastrous for the joint family. Feminist criticism is most suitable for the analysis of this play. M.K. Naik makes a pertinent observation when he says,

> The woman question is presented in greater detail in *Bravely Fought the Queen*. The "Queen" is, of course, the Rani of Jhansi, who died fighting the British in 1857. (The title is derived from a famous Hindi poem, which has the refrain, "*khoob ladi mardani*—the manly queen fought bravely".) Her name is invoked as an ironic parallel to the women in the play who are passive, helpless victims of male tyranny. All the three women in the play suffer, each in her own way. Old Baa's husband has abandoned her, in favour of another woman. She now lies bed-ridden and aged, and no one responds to her call when she rings the bell to summon someone for help. The irony is, it is in her house that his sons and their families are living. Dolly, Baa's elder daughter-in-law, is a pale, meek creature. She is beaten up by her brutal husband, when she is in an advanced stage of pregnancy, so that her daughter is born deformed. Alka, the other daughter-in-law, has her own cross to bear: her husband is a homosexual. The two sons of Baa, Jiten and Nitin are both failed businessmen, and the bonsai plant which appears in the play more than once is an apt symbol of the two young men. (Naik and Narayan 207)

Dattani exposes the hypocritical nature of men who are either harsh to their wives in particular and female sex in general or who betray their wives by being 'gay' and 'bisexual' at the same time. Dattani has the courage of conviction to expose the inherent weakness of human nature with accuracy and objectivity.

In *Tara* Dattani depicts another kind of discrimination against woman (i.e. a girl child). It is here that the mother prefers a son to a daughter and in the process caused the death of the girl. This play can be read profitably if we apply feminist and humanistic criticism to it. With two children (twin) born with three legs between them—two on the girl's side with regular blood-flow and one on the boy's side, the family took a decision to operate them giving two legs to the boy and one to the girl. The result was disastrous. Tara died and Chandan was amputated. In retrospect Chandan thinks it a sin to deprive his sister of her right to live.

It is an irony of fate that the person who was responsible for Tara's plight is not her father but her own mother. The exchange between Tara's father, Patel and mother Bharati makes things clear.

> Patel (*grabs Tara*). Look at her, Bharati. And tell her that you love her very much.
>
> Bharati. Tara knows it. Leave her alone!
>
> Tara. Daddy....
>
> Patel. Tara, please believe me when I say that I love you very much and I have never in all my life loved you less or more than I have loved your brother. But your mother.... (*CP* 354)

The play shows the good matured brother repenting for his sister's death. He seeks the forgiveness of his sister and wants to be united with her. Chandan's emotional appeal for union with his sister redeems the injustice done to her by their mother.

> But somewhere, sometime, I look up at a shooting star...and wish. I wish that a long-forgotten person would forgive me. Wherever she is. And will hug me. Once again. (*CP* 380)

Clearing the Rubble is a play on human condition made precarious by earthquake. It is written against the backdrop of 2001 earthquake in Gujarat. An English journalist revisits the place and looks for the boy he saved by making him free from the rubble. The play is in three voices. It shows the gap between law and human misery and calls for a drastic change in our attitude to help the people in distress. Salim tells Jeffrey the difficulties about getting government compensation in a tone marked by anger and frustration. He says,

> Jeffrey. We stay on because our lives and deaths haven't been acknowledged. The government offers compensation to those who have lost their loved ones only if they can show proof that they lived and died. For those of us who were buried or cremated before a doctor could reach us, we have no proof that we did exist. It is not enough that my mother tells them 'I had three

> children, I lost them all.' It is not enough that our neighbours tell them 'Yes I knew her children, they did exist!' The whole village can scream at them saying 'We did exist! We did live!' That is not enough. Jeffrey, I am sorry. I followed you. Outside my village I existed only in your mind. All of us, want to leave our mark behind. Even if only on a piece of paper in a government office, if not an impression on some unknown person's mind. That the ones we leave behind can say, yes I had a son, here is the proof! I lost two of my daughters, here is the proof! Proof that we existed!... Now that my mother has proof that we did live and you know that we did live, I need not stay on. Goodbye, Jeffrey. (*CP* II 82)

The irony is unmistakable. Dattani has an insight into human nature and that is why his portrayal of human condition is both authentic and moving. He 'sees like steadily and sees it whole', as Eliot would put it.

Ek Alag Mausam (*A Different Season*) is really a different kind of play on the latest dreaded disease HIV positive (AIDS). To write a play on AIDS victims and the reactions of the people to them is to bring alive the contemporary society which shows the predicament of human lives against the onslaught of this disease. Reader-Response criticism can be applied to this play to unfold human agony as well as selfishness of other people who avoid such diseased persons as untouchables. In this play a number of people are affected by this disease and Dattani shows how they live in the society knowing that their days are numbered. Aparna got the disease from her husband, Suresh and George got it through the transfusion of blood from his friend. Other patients got it from other sources like a child getting the virus from infected mother.

What is important in the play is the plight of the HIV positives on whose faces death stares each moment. It is a death-in-life situation which needs human compassion to soothe and assuage their feelings. The conversation of Aparna and George brings home the truth:

George. I am not talking about the time when we won't be here. I am talking about now. All these years that we have left in us. We can be there for each other.

Aparna. To watch each other die? I see my mother observing my every move. My every cough, my every sneeze is painful to her. I can see the terror in her eyes when she is thinking this is the beginning of the end. I can't do this to anyone else. And what makes you think that just because we are both HIV positive, we will be happy together?

George. Forget for a moment that we are HIV. Forget that we have five, seven, ten, twelve years to live. Forget that and then think of our lives together.

Aparna. How can I forget? It is there! Written in our medical reports. Our death warrant. We can have those tests done over and over again but the truth is we will one day have Aids! (*CP* II 533)

The reaction of George's father is in a way the reaction of most of the people and their attitude to victims. George's father tells George harshly in his face to leave them. He makes his son responsible for the humiliation they get from the villagers. Here, the instince of Self-survival takes a precedence over love and affection. This proves the hallowness of human relationship.

In the end, Dattani creates new situation in which Dr Machado makes an appeal to the public to change their attitude to HIV positives. The play ends with a hope that we may conquer AIDS as we have done other diseases in the past. "Today the world over doctors and scientists are trying to find a cure for Aids. In the interest of mankind we hope they succeed. While waiting for that cure to be invented or discovered, let us not forget—that miracles are known to happen." This is the keynote of the play. Writing a play on a sensitive topic like HIV positive virus is to fight for a cause. Dattani has done it well.

Mahesh Dattani's plays have variety, and the themes are of contemporary interest. He has dived deep into human heart and re-created characters with authenticity and a sense of liveliness. To read his plays is to imagine the plight of individuals pining for same-sex love and pleading for legal sanction for their marriage. Gender and Queer theorists support the cause of same-sex love saying that it is as natural as love based on heterosexual relationship. Dattani exposes the fundamentalists and orthodox persons who use religion as a cover (or mask) to realize their selfish interest. Religion is a mere ploy in their hands to further their interest in life and cherish their desired goal. Art and dramatic performances are also used internationally to hoodwink people to cherish the sexual and material desire of some cunning persons with criminal bent of mind. Dattani also writes on human tragedy caused by droughts and healing touch given by some compassionate individuals. Above all, Dattani also glorifies the art form and dance as performing arts which transform human soul and make them humane and noble. But when all is said and done, it appears that in most of his plays Dattani not only deals with common and ordinary people but the common problems of these people in realistic terms. Therefore, we may say that most of his plays are 'Kitchen sink' dramas.

WORKS CITED

Abrams, M.H. "What is a Humanistic Criticism?" *Journal of Literary Criticism,* 8:2, Dec. 1996.

Butler, Judith. From Bodies that Matter (1993) Ed. Rice, Philip and Patricia Waugh. *Modern Literary Theory: A Reader.* New York: OUP, 2001.

Dattani, Mahesh. *Collected Plays.* New Delhi: Penguin Books, 2000.

———. *Collected Plays,* Vol. II. New Delhi: Penguin Books, 2005.

Edgar, Andrew and Peter Sedgwick. *Key Concepts in Cultural Theory.* London: Routledge, 2004.

Murfin, Ross and Supriya M. Ray. *The Bedford Glossary of Critical and Literary Terms.* New York: Bedford Books, 1998.

Naik, M.K. and Shyamala A. Narayan. *Indian English Literature: 1980-2000.* New Delhi: Pencraft International, 2002.

Techniques in Mahesh Dattani's Plays

6

Mahesh Dattani is a theatre personality. Not only he writes plays but also directs them. And what is more, he conducts and organizes workshops on play-writing and stage production. That is how, he has gathered vast experience on the dramatic art and stage craft. The innovations he has made in the area of themes made him popular both at home and abroad. In order to make his characters life-like on the stage, he too made certain innovations in the techniques of his plays. To make the inner thought in the minds of his characters, he introduced the technique of 'thought' instead of 'asides' in his plays. 'Thought' is followed by "Speech" in commensurate with the themes of the play. There is a lot of code-mixing (i.e. Indian words, Hindi words, for example written in English spelling without making an attempt at translation, even when translation is available) in his plays. In this chapter, an attempt has been made to analyse the techniques employed in his plays. In his 'preface' to *Collected Plays* (2000) Dattani states:

> I know that I am an artist. I don't need to underline it in my works. I write for my plays to be performed and appreciated by as wide a section of the society that my plays seek to and are about.... I am certain that my plays are a true reflection of my times, place and socio-economic background. (XIII-XV)

As a playwright Dattani was influenced by Edward Albee's *Who's Afraid of Virginia Woolf?* when he read it in his teens and opined that "it unleashed in me an ability to set up my male and female characters against each other".

There is a vital difference between drama and other forms of literature. Unlike other genres, say poetry, fiction and essays, drama is a performing art. Hence, technique matters a lot in a play. Dattani says,

> I see myself as a craftsman and not as a writer. To me, being a playwright is about seeing myself as a part of the process of a production. I write plays for the sheer pleasure of communicating through this dynamic medium. (Nair 2001, qtd in Chaudhuri 98)

What matters most in a play or drama is performance. Julian Hilton, a theorist, almost discards the audience and the text and concentrates on the performance of the characters. Hilton writes:

> ...in the theatre any plot or action exists only in the moment or performance and has no stable meaning or identity outside of the performance process.... There is no single or necessary definition of what plot or action is, even in the case of a play with an authoritative source 'text'. "For every performance, re-defines however marginally, the nature of the performers." The purpose of performing this becomes the one generating an intensified experience for all who participate in it rather than the representation of some pre-existing action or state of feeling according to some immanent ideal in its poetic textual source, (Hilton 7)

Mahesh Dattani believes in the magic of the spoken word and therefore lays emphasis on the performance of his characters. In the 'Preface' to *Collected Plays* he says,

> Every time the audiences (Critics too!) have applauded, cried or simply offered their silence in response to some moment, in the play, I am completely aware that it is my character that has done the work for me. (XI)

In Dattani's plays, characters play the vital role to reach out to the audience. The themes, rather unusual themes like homosexuality, bi-sexuality, lesbianism, disease like HIV positives (Aids) are brought home to the audience through the acting of the characters—not through the words on the page. To see Dattani's characters acting on the stage is to be aware of contemporary reality that stares us in our face. Dattani says, "If you look at my plays, you would find that each character, every character has, you know his or her space in the play, which an actor can develop" (Katyal 2000, qtd in Chaudhuri 104). Since the emphasis is not on printed words but on the utterance of words through the mouth of characters, Dattani takes a play as a craft. He explains:

> I write to do plays...that is probably where my strength lie, because...as productions they work. [The content is]...definitely a part of my world.... What I see around and within me...I think its craft. Craft first and craft next. That's what theatre is about. (Chauduri 104)

A good example of stagecraft we come across in "Tara". Here the protagonist appropriates to himself the role of the dramatist. Dan's opening dialogue in 'Tara' is significant.

> In poetry, even the most turbulent emotions can be recollected when one is half asleep. But in drama! Ah! Even tranquility has to be recalled with emotion. Like touching a bare live wire. Try distancing yourself from that experience and writing about it! A mere description will be hopelessly inadequate. And for me.... I have to relieve that charge over and over again. (*CP* 323)

Asha Kuthari Chaudhuri makes a valid observation on this point

> In a telling use of an almost choric voice, Dattani uses the god-like doctor's commentary that runs parallel with the memories, wherever required, the introductions being mockingly performed by Dan, now an interviewer on television. There is another effective reference to drama in the parallel that is drawn by Dr Thakkar between the surgical procedure that he orchestrates and the theatricality echoing through it, putting to good use the suggestion in the word 'operation theatre': 'We had had about six rehearsals with dummies to make sure that every detail was considered, in terms of the physical movements of the surgeons during the operation as well as surgical procedure'". (*CP* 363)

When Dan finally gets out of the act of the interviewer, he says,

> Yes. The material is there. But the craft is yet to come. Like the amazing Dr Thakkar, I must take from Tara and give it to myself. Make capital of my trauma, my anguish, and make it my tragedy. To masticate them in my mind and spit out the result to the world, an anger. (*CP* 379)

The finger he points at the artist is perhaps an indictment, perhaps merely a revelation to the self, but the point Dattani is making, clearly shows one of the least considered, 'invisible' issues in art-making artistic 'capital' out of angst, sorrow, or feelings of the subjects... (108-09).

Again Dattani uses his 'voice-over' techniques to bring in the authorial note through the mouth of his protagonist, Dan. This is how the play moves towards its end.

> Dan (Voice-over). Someday, after I die, a stranger will find this recording and play it. The voice is all that will remain. No writing. No masterpiece. Only a voice—that once belonged to an object. An object like other objects in a cosmos, whose orbits are determined by those around. Moving in a forced harmony. Those who survive are those who do not defy the gravity of others. And those who desire even a moment of freedom, find themselves hurled into space, doomed to crash with some unknown force. (*Pause.*) I no longer desire that freedom. I move, just move, without meaning. I forget Tara. I forget that I had a sister—with whom I had shared a body. In one comfortable womb. Till we were forced out...and separated.
>
> *A spot faded in—empty.*
>
> But somewhere, sometime, I look up at a shooting star...and wish. I wish that a long-forgotten person would forgive me. Wherever she is.
>
> *Tara walks into the spot without limping. Dan also appears without the limp.*
>
> And will hug me. Once again.
>
> *They kneel, face to face.*
>
> Forgive me, Tara. Forgive me for making it my tragedy. (*CP* 379-80)

Dattani's portrayal of Dan's character brings to our mind the perceptive observation of Kenneth Pickering on drama:

> When we speak of a 'character' in a play we think of them as a living person but, in reality, until an actor begins to work on the play, the character is nothing more than a series of speeches and stage directions on the page. What a character says and how he or she says it are major features of bringing a play to life and will determine the way in which a performer conceives the person he or she is portraying. (44-45)

In *Where There's a Will*, Dattani makes the principal character, Hasmukh Mehta say his feelings directly to the audience even after his death. Both in life and in death, Mehta speaks the text directly to the audience because the play exists in its performance. His agony springs from his inability to set his house in order in his life-time and therefore, he wants to do it through his Mistress, Kiran after his death. No wonder, he speaks aloud in this beginning of the play.

> Have you ever noticed how women are all alike in their behaviour? For instance, if you ask them whether breakfast or lunch or dinner is ready, they always say 'Yes'. And it never really is ready. An hour ago, before going for my walk, I asked my wife the same question—'If dinner ready.' And she said. (*Imitates Sonal.*) 'Yes'. And it still isn't. I expected my daughter-in-law to have more sense. But what did she say when I asked her the same question? You heard her. (*Imitates Preeti.*) 'Yes'. But she is an intelligent girl, I can tell you. She has her eye on my money. Why else would she agree to marry a dead loss like my son. (*Lights a cigarette.*) My son isn't really after my wealth. That's because he doesn't have any brains. (*Smokes.*) I shouldn't be smoking these. Doctor's orders. I've got high blood pressure, high cholesterol. I also have an enlarged heart. In the old days, if you said someone had a large heart, you meant he was generous and loving. Today it means he is receiving high aggravation from his twenty-three-year-old son and his scheming daughter-in-law. (*Puffs on his cigarette.*) At the rate I'm puffing. I should be dead in forty minutes. (*CP* 456)

Since Hasmukh was unhappy with his wife Sonal, he had a mistress. But what is important is that he made a Will in the name of his mistress, Kiran to teach his son Ajit, daughter-in-law, Preeti, a lesson. As the stage direction shows, Hasmukh is sitting cross-legged on the dining table and speach to the audience. Dattani makes configuration of time, speech and movement in the character of Hasmukh.

> Hasmukh (to the audience). Have you ever swung on a tamarind tree? Upside down? You should try it some time. You can see the world the way it really is. It's important to get a good grip on the branch with your legs. Then you can relax your hands and head. Like this (*Demonstrates by lying on his back and letting his head and hands dangle over the side of the table*). How do I look? I don't know about me, but you all definitely look peculiar. (*Points at someone.*) Your shoes need polishing. (*Straightens up*) That's the way I see my family now. Their lives have been turned upside down since Kiran entered this house. I suppose it was a nasty thing to do. Making Kiran come and live here. You may ask—what kind of a fool would ask his mistress to live with his family? A fool who knows his family very well. Kiran may have been my mistress, but she has far more brains than my wife ever had. But you should see her now, my wife! Transformed. From stupid incapable housewife to cover incapable housewife. Every day is a new lesson for her on husband-undertaking. The more time she spends with Kiran, the more she learns about me. The most she learns about me, the most she'll regret having been such a good-for-nothing wife. That will keep her from being a happy widow ever after. One thing I can't stand is a happy widow. There should be a law against them. (*Pause. He resumes his cross-legged position.*) There's one more reason why I want Kiran here. To keep a check on my daughter-in-law. If there's anyone who has me worried, it's her. She is a clever piece. Might find some loophole in the will. But Kiran is too clever for her. Any woman who is a mistress and a wife has to be clever. (*CP* 496)

The text quoted above, could pass for a soliloquy. Since, dead Hasmukh is talking to the audience directly, we may call it as a soliloquy in death.

Hasmukh also speaks directly to his wife and mistress after his death. By making dead Hasmukh speak directly to living characters, Dattani wants to bring the subconscious mind of the dead protagonist to the surface to say what he thought when he was alive. For example, when Kiran impresses upon Sonal that one has to learn to give if they want to get anything in life, Sonal replies, "And I never got because I never gave". Pat came dead Hasmukh response:

> Bravo! That's what I wanted to hear! (Dances) She has learnt her lesson! She has learnt her lesson! (To the audience) Now you can go home and I can go to heaven. (*CP* 507)

When Hasmukh's family got reconciled to Kiran's staying with them permanently, he became very happy. Let's examine the following dialogues:

> Kiran. We have to remain friends for another twenty-one years.
>
> Sonal. Not for twenty-one-years. For ever!
>
> Hasmukh. No. I don't think I can enter this house.
>
> It isn't mine...anyone. I will rest permanently on the tamarind tree. They are not family any more. I wish I had never interfered with their lives. They look quite happy together with Kiran sitting in my place. Oh, I wish I had been more...I wish I had lived. (*CP* 515)

In *Bravely Fought the Queen,* Dattani makes use of a new technique to bring out the discrimination against woman. Here the play is less in the text but more on acting and performance. In the introduction to the play, Michael Walling writes:

> This is a play about performances; and uses the theatre to demonstate how, in a world of hypocrisy, acting becomes a way of life. Paradoxically, it is only by the overt performance of the theatre that such acting can be exposed for what it is. For example, when Dolly reveals the fact that her child was seriously disabled at birth by Jiten's violence, she begins to

dance as Daksha would dance—disjointedly, wildly, with ever-increasing frenzy, until at least she breaks down in a gut-wrenching grief. Every night, as I watched this extraordinary moment, I was moved by its deep theatrical purity. Siddiqua Akhtar was performing as Dolly; Dolly as Daksha; Daksha was performing a dance. By exploiting layer upon layer of performance, of unreality, Mahesh allowed his actress a route to emotion in its rawest form: the pain, the anguish in the blood-knot of the family which is his constant theme. (*CP* 230)

So far as technique is concerned, Dattani lays emphasis on four words: 'Silence', 'stillness', 'sound' and 'movement'. Characters in intricate situations remain 'silent' and continue in 'stillness' for a moment, then speak out—that is, 'sound' and finally make the movement. This varies from play to play. All these four—'silence', 'stillness', 'sound' and 'movement'—are brilliantly worked out in *Dance Like a Man.*

Here, Dattani brings reconciliation between the Dancing couple, Jairaj and Ratna in the end, by transcending the time after they were shocked to know that their son was given opium by the ayah. This is how Dattani presents the scene before the audience:

Jairaj (gets up). What do you mean?

A low beat on the mridangam is heard. Ratna looks at him terror-stricken. Jairaj advances towards her.

What did you say? She too has given "Shankar"? (*Grabs Ratna.*) What did you say? She too has given Shankar? (*Lets go of her.*) You?

RATNA (screaming). No!

Jairaj rushes up the stairs. Ratna looks up and slowly goes up the stairs as music plays. The lights dim. She exists hurriedly. The music culminates in a stream which comes from the older Ratna. The garden changes into the living room. The music however continues, perhaps muted. The lights remain subdued. The older Ratna comes down the stairs almost in a trance. The older Jairaj enters, and stands in shadows, watching her as she sits down. He moves and

> *stands beside her. They are both fixed in a spotlight. All sense of time is abandoned now.* (CP 446)

Thereafter they vacated the flat which went to Lata and Viswas. The play ends with Jairaj's dialogue in the following manner:

> *The younger Jairaj strikes a post. The younger Ratna laughs and hits him playfully.*
>
> Today my liver ceased to function. And I followed suit. You died too. Out of boredom, I suspect. Our flat is empty now. It belongs to Lata and Viswas. I see you coming to what seems to be heaven, riding with Death on a buffalo. You get off and I greet you. The buffalo vanishes. (*Flute.*) And we embrace. We smile. And we dance.
>
> *The younger Jairaj and Ratna smile and embrace.*
>
> We dance perfectly. In unison. Not missing a step or a beat. We talk and laugh at all the mistakes we made in our previous dances.
>
> *The younger Ratna strikes a pose which the younger, Jairaj seems to disagree with.*
>
> We were only human. We lacked the grace. We lacked the brilliance. We lacked the magic to dance like God.
>
> *The younger couple is ready to dance and salute the audience while the music builds up and the spotlights fade.* (CP 447)

Dance is a performing art and what matters most here are 'silence', and 'movement'. Expression of the dancer is mostly through 'silence', 'stillness' and finally 'movement'. Dance is a divine art. Men and women can dance but very rarely they achieve perfection in it. That is why the title of the play is 'Dance Like a Man'. In dance perfection lies with gods. They dance and through it express their thoughts, words don't matter. It is rightly said that Lord Shiva is the perfect dancer. That is why, Dattani ends his play with an honest admission that 'we lacked the magic to dance like god'.

The technique of 'thought' and 'voice-over' is clearly shown in the play "Do the Needful". The old method of 'aside' is done away with. What the character thinks and tells to the audience, is kept as a secret from the character spoken to. For examples, Lata who is in love with Salim, keeps it a secret from Alpesh and her parents. Similarly, Alpesh who has homosexual relationship with Trilok, keeps it a secret from Lata and others. Reacting to her marriage proposal. Late lapses into 'thought'. Here are a few examples:

> Lata (*thought*). Salim. I know you are allowed four wives—what's the point in thinking of all that now? I will have to be content keeping you as a lover. How are we going to work this out? What if you have to go back to Kashmir?... I will have to find another lover. I can have more than four.... Why do I think all this? I am a bad girl, I will rot in hell. Oh! Damn the Bangalore Catholic School, sending me on a guilt trip now. (*CP* 126-27)
>
> Lata (*thought.*) Salim. I really wanted to cry, whine, do anything to stop it all from happening. Mummy was quicker.
>
> Lata (*thought.*) This was the bit I hated. The last buffalo complained about my narrow hips. Honestly, I would have screamed if this one had done that. You don't need wide hips to bear children, for God's sake". (*CP* 132)

Alpesh being gay, is not interested in marrying Lata. He is also not happy with his parents' indulging in big talks about his business to Lata's parents. This is how Dattani presents his mind through 'thought' in the following lines:

> Alpesh (*thought.*) What could I say to them? Daddy had his colleague approve the loan. We paid enough bribes to get the damn thing off. We hired the underworld to have Grandpa's tenants evicted.... I hate lying' and liars. I have to do it so often. I feel every time I speak, I am lying. (*Pause.*) In case you think I am rich.... I am just the caretaker. (*CP* 136)
>
> Alpesh (*thought.*) What could I say, Trilok? How would I tell her to reject me?
>
> Alpesh (*thought.*) She was waiting for me to say something. May be I should have told her about you. After all, she was decent enough to bring up her Salman or Salim or whatever. (*CP* 149)

> Alpesh (*thought*): Trilok.
>
> Lata (*thought*) Salim. I will be meeting you soon. I hope you understand. You had better. At least with you, I can be more honest. And demanding. (*CP* 156)

In an e-mail reply to the present author, Dattani wrote that in radio drama, thoughts are processed differently in recording, so the need to differentiate between what is a 'voice-over' or sutradhar or inner thought. This techniques suits some of his plays as they were broadcast first before printed as dramatic texts. That technique also does away with 'asides' and 'soliloques' traditionally used in plays.

The same technique of 'thought' followed by 'voice-over' is employed in *Seven Steps Around the Fire,* a play devoted to the theme of the plight of hijras in our society. Uma, the researcher, ruminates about the origin of hijras and their plight in the society in her 'thought' in the following words:

> Uma *(thought).* Nobody seems to know anything about them. Neither do they. Did they come to this country with Islam, or are they a part of our glorious Hindu tradition? Why are they so obsessed with weddings and ceremonies of childbirth? How do they come to know of these wedding? Why do they just show up without being invited? Are they just extortionists? And why do they not take singing lessons?
>
> (*Pause*) Is it true? Could it be true what my mother used to say about them? Did they really put a curse on her because they did not allow them to sing and dance at their wedding? Or was that their explanation for not being able to have children of their own? (*CP* 16-17)
>
> Uma (*thought*). Then is it true? That they are criminals? Am I making a food or myself? Even so, I've got to find out for myself.... Who knows? (*CP* 17)

The play ends with Uma's thought in the form of "voice-over" as quoted below:

> Uma (*Voice-over*). They knew. Anarkali, Champa and all the hijra people knew who was behind the killing of Kamla. They have no voice. The case was hushed up and was not

> even reported in the newspapers. Champa was right the police made no arrests. Subbu's suicide was written off as an accident. The photograph was destroyed. So were the lives of two young people. (*CP* 42)

The same technique of 'thought', followed by 'voice-over' is found in "Clearing the Rubble". This play begins with the thoughts of three persons, Salim, Jeffrey and Fatima against, the backdrop of massive earthquake that devasted the land of Kutch in Gujarat. The journalist, Jeffrey, undertakes the journey for the second time to meet the boy, Salim. Fatima's agony is expressed in her thought in the following words:

> Allah be merciful! It is time for my prayer. Forgive me, but I cannot face Mecca. I cannot move. My Allah, please forgive me! Please show compassion. Both my daughters are with you now. I am coming too. Take me away from this unjust world now. I will hold the bodies of my daughters till I follow them to your world. I have no more strength to call out to those people who help others but not us. I cry out for you now. Only in your world is there justice. I want to be in your world. (*CP* II 65)

Earthquakes victims feel that they have been denied justice by the government when Nature has devasted them. It is the injustice both of Nature and the Government that caused agony in the hearts of people. All their reactions are reflected in theirs thoughts. Hence, the technique of 'thought' and 'voice-over' well-suited Dattani. Take for example, Salim's 'thought' which explains the whole situation:

> (*Thought*) Jeffrey.... This is not my village any more. It has withstood many calamities. Droughts, floods, caste wars. But the earthquake that brought you here, took my village some place else. In my mind it is a peaceful village. Nothing much happens here. We are born, we live, we die.... No different from other places. But for those who live here, it is the center of the universe. This is where I belong, with the ghost of my village. You cannot even speak my language and I can only tell you so much in yours. For those who lived here, we knew no other universe. This was our world. You

> may not understand my words as I speak them now. (*CP* II 79-80)

Irony is an important mode to expose the injustice prevalent in the society. Therefore, the 'thought' of the characters are expressed in irony giving the impetus to the theme of the play. Dattani questions, though implicitly, the method of giving compensation to the victims of the devasting earthquake in the character of Salim. Salim, in a voice charged with emotion tells:

> Jeffrey. We stay on because our lives and deaths haven't been acknowledged. The government offers compensation to those who have lost their loved ones only if they can show proof that they lived and died. For those of us who were buried or cremated before a doctor could reach us, we have no proof that we did exist. It is not enough that my mother tells them, 'I had three children, I lost them all.' It is not enough that our neighbours tell them, 'Yes I knew her children, they did exist!' The whole village can scream at them saying 'We did exist! We did love!' That is not enough. (*CP* II 82)

Elaborate stage direction is an important device of Dattani's plays. Through state directions, Dattani explains the situation of the plays and the moods of the characters. In "Thirty Days in September", Shanta and Mala (mother and daughter) are depicted as victims of sexual exploitation by their blood relationships. The theme of incest is central to the play. Mala's taped conversation given in stage direction and her phone call explain their plight.

Thus, Dattani writes:

> During Mala's taped conversation, we see the back of a life-sized doll of a seven-year-old girl propped on a chair. During the first conversation we only see the back of the head. With the first conversation we only see the back of the head with every subsequent taped conversations, we see more of the profile.... (*CP* II 7)

> Mala's voice on tape. I have been so bad, I can't tell you where to begin! It's not just the man in the office I told you about, but before...much before! I—Oh God! I—I seduced

my uncle when I was thirteen! I—slept with my cousin—and—anyone who was available.... (*CP* II 33)

When Mala learns about the trauma, her mother had undergone during her childhood, she forgives her mother. The union between the daughter and the mother becomes a foregone conclusion. Dattani aptly closed the play in the following manner:

> Mala. While I accused you of not recognizing my pain, you never felt any anger at me for not recognizing yours. We were both struggling to survive but—I never acknowledged your struggle. Ma, no matter where I am, I always think of you. I want you to know that I am listening. Waiting for you to speak. I promise you I will listen. I am waiting for a sign from you...to say that you have forgiven me. Say something. Even a whisper.
>
> *The scrim wall around the prayer room rises. Mala is overjoyed. Shanta continues with her prayer. Mala walks up to her and kneels.*
>
> I just want to...I want to ask you whether you need my help. Please let me be of help. (*Gently turning her mother's face towards her.*) It's not your fault, mother. Just as it wasn't my fault. Please, tell me that you've forgiven me for blaming you. Please tell me that.
>
> *Shanta turns back to her God and continues with her prayers. Mala slowly rests her head in Shanta's tap.*
>
> Mala. I know you will, mother. I know you have.
>
> *Shanta picks up the bell and begins to ring it even as the lights fade out.* (*CP*, 58)

The last quoted line given in the form of stage direction is ambiguous. May be, Shanta has forgiven Mala and accepted her. Or, may be, she has turned to God discarding the human bond between the mother and the daughter. We may say like Shakespeare's Othello, 'it is better as it is'.

In *The Swami and Winston*, Dattani does not give stage directions in an elaborate way—he only says about 'Exterior' when things happen outside and 'interior', when things happen inside the house. In a straightforward language he states how religion is used as a tool to further one's personal interest. Two extracts given below show how the hypocritical people use religion as a play and how they are exposed in the long run:

> Sitaram Trivedi. There are two types of Europeans. Ones who understand and appreciate the depth and complexity of Hindu philosophy and the others who feel threatened by it. The world will realize the greatness of the Hindu way of life. Wait and see. It is a question of time. They can't be blind for ever even if they choose not to see. They have to open their eyes sooner or later. We shall have our temples all over the world. (*CP* II 303)

> Uma. ...by framing the Swami, he would get rid of an opposer. The Swami is truly spiritual and wants none of this new brand of Hinduism. Radha was totally under her father's control, it would be very easy for Sitaram Trivedi to manage the property once she inherits it from Charles whom I am sure he would have killed in a way to make it look like an accident. He had grand plans. England would have been the perfect place to set up his own pseudo ashram. (*CP* II 325)

Dattani's plays read like real life stories, only the names of characters are changed. To read or watch his plays is to transport ourselves to the contemporary world of which we are a part.

In *Morning Raga,* Dattani gives elaborate stage directions to show how personal relationship between individuals can be transcended through music. In this play, Swarnalatha, a carnatic singer had a desire to sing in a city, which could not materialize earlier because of the death of her friend who was a singer and Abhinay's mother. It was Abhinay who with the help of Pinkie brings Swarnalatha's desire to fruition in the end.

The ending of the play has elaborate stage directions in which through the flashback technique Dattani brings a union between the dead and the living by the music performance of Swarnalatha. The play has a significant and suggestive ending:

> Swarnalatha. Thank you. It has been a difficult raga for me to learn. Twenty years is a long time. Music is a never ending journey.

It has been my dream to sing for an audience such as you. But... (*Finding it difficult to get the words.*) tonight, I will sing this song for my son who, like my music, has returned after a very long journey. (*Looking at Abhinay.*) Abhinay, I sing this raga for you—my son.

Another spotlight picks up Abhinay who is so touched by this tribute. Swarnalatha begins to sing once again. Abhinay picks up his violin and begins to play. Pinkie joins in on the English Lyrics. The three are lit in individual follow spots. Swarnalatha looks at Abhinay as he plays. A flashback of Swarnalatha imagining singing this song to her son. They are playing by the river. Abhinay when he plays the violin.... A flashback where Abhinay imagines his mother Vaishnavi singing and playing with him. Pinkie sings and imagines (flashback) her father rocking her to sleep. The three of them come together in one spot. Flashback of Swarnalatha and her son, Vaishnavi and young Abhinay running in slow motion across the bridge. The song ends to a thunderous applause. They take their bows and look at each other. The music picks up as the credits roll. (*CP* II 417)

In *Uma and the Fairy Queen*, Dattani uses the phone call of a character when he/she is alone to reveal important information. This can be taken as a substitute for dramatic monologue. Uma's phone call to Charles about the staging of the play, after Michael's supposed kidnapping and sudden reappearance is a good example of dramatic monologue under a different name. Again Uma's phone to Mr Menon and Mumtaz to know the past of Nila and her activities can be taken as Dattani's new method of handling a dramatic monologue. This is how the phone call goes:

Uma. Hellow, Mr Menon?... this is Uma Rao, my husband is the Superintendent of Police, I think the Commissioner spoke to you about me...good.... Yes I do have a copy of the reports, thank you. There is just something that I want a clarification on...it's to do with the note, is that the only scrap you have or am I missing a copy of something?... I see...and one more question for now. It says there were three sets of fingerprints found on the note and one set belongs to a woman and one of the deceased, anything on the criminal records matching the third?.... When will you know?.... Thank you so much. I appreciate your cooperation.

She hangs up.

(*Contemplating.*) These are the forgeries of jealousy?

She dials again.

Hellow? Mumtaz?... (*Laughing.*) Yes, it is! How are you?... I wish I was, except now they have made it so difficult for us to get a visa to Pakistan!... Yes, it's awful all this talk and diplomatic one upmanship.... Mumtaz, I was doing some research for a magazine and I thought I could use your help. I couldn't find anything much on the internet. Remember Nila Ahmed?... The TV star, yes.... OH! You read about it? Yes it's awful. Right here in my hometown... (*Laughing*). You are clever. Yes I must admit I am doing some sleuthing on that...oh good. To start with, what's the name of the serial she acted in? The one that made her really famous?... (*Scribbling down on paper.*) Right.... No I never got to see it. We didn't get it here...(*Scribbling down the name.*) Wasn't she married when she met Michael?... But Ahmed is really her screen name? What then was her married name? I see...Tell me, there was some scandal about her wasn't there?... Hmmmm. There was quite a bit of gossip around her I remember.... Oh.... Right, it's coming back. (*CP* II 445-46)

The mingling of reality and imagination is given in the form of stage directions in *Ek Alag Mausam*, a play written on the HIV positives. Aparna, a HIV positive, which she got from her husband, meets George, a truck driver another, HIV positive who fails in love with her. These two situations are brought together through the following technique:

Flash of George driving truck, Surreal.

Aparna swerves to avoid the truck, spilling the orange juice. The truck driver honks madly at her and drives on. She pulls over to the side of the road and stops the car. Aparna reaches out for some tissue and begins wiping the seats. She gets out of the car to wipe off the stain on her sari. Paro gets out too and walks away from the car. Aparna looks at Paro sitting under a tree. Aparna sighs and leans against the car.

Cut to:

Interior, Aparna's home, Surreal.

Suresh is lying on the sofa with his arm covering his face.

Aparna walks in through the main doorway.

Aparna. Suresh! (Going to the sofa) Suresh! It is confirmed. I am pregnant!

Suresh mumbles something and rolls over and goes to sleep.

Aparna picks up the bottle of rum that has fallen down and props it on the table. (*CP* II 475)

HIV positive being a fatal disease, death is inevitable. Even then, the HIV positives want to live in. The whole world and our life move with the Sun. This beautiful image of the Sun as a ball in God's Hand has been employed by Dattani in the following lines:

And the Sun is his ball. When he kicks the ball, it is Sunrise.
The ball goes high in the air. That is noon.

When it lands in the goal, it is sunset.

God always scores a goal. (*CP* II 556)

The Tale of a Mother Feeding Her Child is a dramatic monologue in a female voice on the theme of human love and compassion. Since it is a radio play, there is no stage directions. The language of the play is evocative of the situation in which the protagonist finds herself and communicates with the strangers from the core of her heart. Let us read the closing paragraph of the play:

I stayed on with them for months. I brought them food from the local sweet shop. Day after day we gorged on samosas, jalebis, kachoris...the whole hut was filled with bottles of mineral water. The postman visited us often and translated for us. We played in the sands, Shanti and I. Jaman's wife and aunt taught me some songs. They laughed at my Hindi. Soon the monsoons arrived. We danced in the rains. I helped them plough their land. We ran through the fields and bathed in the pond. Mother Earth's breasts were swelling up once again with nourishment for her children. I could have

> stayed on forever. But I had to come back to Jennifer. I got a call from the hospital....
>
> I saved them. At least I saved Shanti. I fed here every day and will do so as long as I live.
>
> I am as helpless with Jennifer as Jaman's wife was with Shanti. There is a veil between us. But it is Jennifer who wears it. She can't see me she can't see herself.... I hope somebody will save my Jennifer. By making her accept my help. She just won't eat. She just won't eat. At least I saved Shanti. (*CP* II 572)

Dattani's lucid prose style is excellent and the poetic language endears him to the readers and audience alike. One feels like returning to it again and again.

Dattani dives deep into human nature and makes certain observations which have universal value and become proverbial lines. Here are a few examples:

(i) He (the musk deer) searches everywhere for the source of the heavenly fragrance, not realizing it is contained within his own body. (*CP* 37)

(ii) A woman in a man's world may be considered being progressive. But a man in a woman's world is pathetic. (*CP* II 140)

(iii) Any food served with love will be tasty. (*CP* 145)

(iv) Everyone is alone in their own cycles of joy and terror. (*CP* 205)

(v) There are things that are better left unsaid. (*CP* 215)

(vi) One can create one's own freedom wherever one may be. (*CP* 220)

(vii) Any woman who is a mistress and a wife has to be clever.

(viii) Damned if you have children, and damned if you don't. (*CP* II 467)

Dattani employs flashback technique in *Morning Raga* to bring the past of Swarnalatha, Vaishnavi and Abhinay to reinforce the present situation in which Swarnalatha being pursued by Abhinay, fulfils her life's ambition.

Mahesh Dattani belongs to a class of its own from the technical point of view. That is because, Dattani being more interested in theatre than in the text lays emphasis on production of the play. In his plays, performance has been given preference to words on the play. Like medium in structuralist criticism, performance is the message in Dattani's plays. No wonder that he has dispensed with the traditional techniques like asides, soliloquies, etc. and brought in 'thought', 'voice-over' and on phone conservation to suit his new themes. The same character's past and present are presented not in terms of flashbacks but as the observation of the same person in two selves—young and old as he has done in the character of Daksha and Hardika in "Final Solutions". Let us examine the following speeches:

Daksha. "Dear Diary, today is the first time I have dared to put my thoughts on your pages...31 March 1948.

Hadrika. After forty years.... I opened my diary again. And I wrote. A dozen pages before. A dozen pages now. A young girl's childish scribble. An old woman's shaky scrawl. (*CP* II 167)

The change in attitude to current problems is brought out by the change in attitude of the old woman, who held a different view of it in her young age. Hence, Dattani introduced a dialogue between two selves (young and old) of the same person under two different names.

Similarly, he made a change, though marginally in the ending of the play, *Dance Like a Man* in (*CP* II). In the second book, Lata is expecting and says if it would be a boy, he would be named Shankar. Dattani changes the closing three lines of the Book I, "We were only human. We lacked the grace. We lacked brilliance. We lacked the magic to dance like God", to only one line in Book II, "Then we had all the grace, all the brilliance, all the magic to dance like the gods." Perhaps, this change is made to inspire the future generation to take to dance as a profession and above all, to carry forward the tradition to its local conclusion.

The time in Dattani's plays is short. The plays are set in the present and the action takes a very limited time—varying from a day to some months. There are flashback techniques as in *Final Solutions* where the old woman goes down the memory lane to recollect her life in her teens. But the play is located in the present. What Peter Szondi speaks in *Theory of the Modern Drama* holds good for Dattani. He says,

> The dramatist is absent from the Drama. He does not speak; he institutes discussion. The drama is not written, it is set. All the lines spoken in the drama are disclosures. They are spoken in context and remain there. They should in no way be perceived as coming from the author. The drama belongs to the author only as a whole, and this connection is just as incidental aspect of its reality as a work. (8)

Dattani's exactly does the same. He raises the issues from sexuality to criminality and then moves on to topical subjects like communal violence, and deadly disease like Aids and allows the characters to express their views freely. The same technique he adopts with reference to subjects like, music, dance and human relationships. The readers and the audience respond to the dialogues uttered by the characters. His plays evoke a good deal of empathy. His theatrical language modifies his dramatic texts and is reflected in the performance of the characters.

Dattani's technique in interior/exterior (to show the characters in their houses and outside), thought/speech (to show what is passing in their mind and how they express it) and elaborate stage directions to make the situations and positions of the actors clear, the straightforward language and code-mixing in some plays where he used Hindi words without translation as in *On a Muggy Night in Mumbai* and *Do the Needful* are innovations in Indian English drama. For subtlety of variations, for sensual opulence, and for technical aptness, Dattani's plays will be enjoyed by both the readers and the play-goers alike.

WORKS CITED

Chaudhury, Asha Kuthari, *Mahesh Dattani*. New Delhi: Foundation Books Pvt. Ltd., 2005.

Dattani, Mahesh. *Collected Plays*. New Delhi: Penguin Books, 2000.

Dattani, Mahesh. *Collected Plays,* Vol. II. New Delhi: Penguin Books, 2005.

Hilton, Julian. *New Directions in Theatre*. London: MacMillan, 1994.

Szondi, Peter. *Theory of the Modern Drama*. Trans. Michael Hays. Cambridge: Polity Press, 1987.

7

Stage Craft

Drama is a performing art. Words in a play do not invite us to react as readers. On the contrary the articulation of words through the mouths of characters thrills us—makes us see into the life of things. It is performance on the stage by the actors that influences the audience. Written words don't matter in a play, as they do or in poetry, or in fiction. That is why, the stage direction, movement and setting of the play matter most in our understanding of the texts. Mahesh Dattani knows it well and acts in that direction.

All his plays are experimented on the stage and some of his plays were staged first and printed afterwards. In a theatre four words matter—they are stillness, silence, sound, and movement. The setting of the play depends on the arrangement of these four which give it a distinct identity. The movement of the characters and events is governed by stillness, silence and sound. Let's see how these things work out in Dattani's plays.

As stated in *Collected Plays* "Seven Steps Around the Fire" was first, broadcast as "Seven Circles Around the Fire" by BBC Radio 4 on 9 January 1999 and was first performed on stage at the Museum Theatre, Chennai, by MTC production and The Madras Players on 6 August 1999. This play has twenty movements from the beginning to the end. It opens with "Interior. The Office of the Superintendent of Police", when Uma, the researcher and Munswamy, the constable arrive there to see the hijra.

Then the play moves to "Interior. The Male Section of Central Jail, Bangalore". Munswamy's words are followed by silence, as they proceed to find out the hijra. The scene shifts to "Interior. The bedroom of Suresh and Uma". Uma goes to the myth in the Ramayana to explain the origin of hijras. From these, the plays moves back to "Interior. The Office of the Superintendent of Police", where we meet Anarkali, a hijra who tells about her relationship with Kamla:

> What is there to tell? I sing with other hijras at weddings and when a child is born. People give us money otherwise I will put a curse on them (Laughs). As if God is on our side (smokes). I did not do anything to Kamla. She was my sister. (*CP* 12)

Then the scene shifts to 'Interior: A car driving through busy roads'. Unlike 'voice-over' in her bedroom, where she spoke of hijra myth in the *Ramayana*, now she keeps the thinking unto herself. Hence, Dattani through the technique of 'thought' dives deep into Uma's mind.

Uma (thought). Nobody seems to know anything about them. Neither do they. Did they come to this country with Islam or are they a part of our glorious Hindu tradition? Why are they so obsessed with weddings and ceremonies of childbirth? How do they come to know of these weddings? Why do they just show up without being invited? Are they just extortionists? And why do they not take singing lessons? (*CP* 16).

Then the scene shifts to Ramaswamy's house, from where Uma speaks to her Vice Chancellor father on phone. She asks her father to give her Rs. 50,000 to buy a present for Mr Sharma's son, Subbu. Again the scene changes and we see the "Exterior. In the Car". Uma goes to visit Champa to enquire about Kamla. We are shown then the "Interior. The living room of Champa". Here Champa tells Uma how Salim used to come there to take Kamla for Subbu. Then the scene changes to Kamla's room. Champa mourns over Kamla's death.

Uma dials the phone in "Interior" to tell her supervisor, why she wants to complete her Ph.D. She says,

> ...I find it more and more difficult to do through research.... I guess I will have to.... If my family throws me out, I hope that doctorate come in handy. (*CP* 28-29)

Dattani highlights a woman's concern for career and economic independence.

From that Dattani takes us to "Exterior: In a Car" and thereafter to "the gates of the minister's residence". As we move on to the living room of Mr. Sharma, the Minister, where the former makes a conversation with Uma. Uma tells the Minister that it is difficult to say who killed Kamla. Again the scene shifts to the bedroom of Suresh and Uma. The wife and husband as usual differ from each other. When Uma wanted to be with Anarkali for sometime. Suresh refused saying 'that would be difficult'.

The scene shifts to "Exterior. Bazzar" where Uma met Champa. And then, they move on to the living room of Champa. Here, Anarkali asked Uma whether the latter would go to the Minister's son's wedding to which she replied in the affirmative. As the scene changes, Suresh and Uma go in a car to Minister's house. In the climactic scene, "At the wedding", Subbu takes the wedding photograph from Anarkali (i.e. his own wedding photo with Kamla) and shoots himself. Then the focus shifts to Champa's living room, where she tells Uma all about Subbu's marriage to Kamla. In the last scene the spot becomes the Office of the Superintendent of Police. Here Uma and Suresh discuss Subbu's death. The play ends with Uma's speech which is very suggestive. The conclusion is appropriate to the unusual theme of the play:

> Uma (voice-over). They knew, Anarkali, Champa and all the hijra people knew who was behind the killing of Kamla. They have no voice. The case was hushed up and was not even reported in the newspapers.... The police made no arrests. Subbu's suicide was written off as an accident. The photograph was destroyed. So were the lives of the young people.... (*CP* 42)

The stage in *On a Muggy Night in Mumbai* has three acting areas: the first is a "small flat, beautifully done up in 'ethnic chic' fashion". Here hangs a picture of Meena Kumari from Pakeezah.

The second areas, as the stage direction reveals is "a completely non-realistic set comprising three levels...characters in this area are immediately suspended in a 'Shoonya' where they are forced to confront their inner thoughts". The third is Kamlesh's bedroom, "hidden behind a gauze wall, giving it some mystery and secrecy". Dattani makes the stage direction clear in the following words:

> The backdrop of these three acting areas is the Mumbai skyline, engulfing the created world of Kamlesh, the secret private space of the bedroom and the deeper space that belongs to the inner thoughts of the character. (*CP* 49)

Dattani successfully re-creates the characters when he allows them to mix their Hindi words with English—that makes their performance real and appealing. The technique of code mixing goes with the movement of the play. Let's take the following conversation between Kamlesh and guard:

> Kamlesh. Tum, Kya ... yeh sab ... paise ke liye karte ho?
>
> Guard. Nahin. (Realizes the implication of what he said, Hastily.) Hahn! Hahn, main paise ke liye hi to karta hoon sab kuch!
>
> Kamlesh. You do enjoy it. What you do to me, what I do to you. Don't you?
>
> Guard. (A little nervously). Ab main jaon?
>
> Kamlesh. But we will have to pretend you do it only for the money!
>
> Guard. Duty Chalu hai, Saab. Secretary daantega mujhe. (*CP* 51)

Kamlesh's sister Kiran, her fiancé Ed, Sharad, a friend of Kamlesh—all assemble here and discuss their private selves. Later on Bunny and Deepali joined them. In Act II the characters remain more or less in the same position. Dattani overtly displays the sexuality of these characters through their actions. The same sex love (homosexuality and lesbianism) may be a reality for some people but that is not the norm of the society. From cultural point of view the same-sex love comes as a shock to people who believe in healthy man-woman relationship leading to procreation and building of family.

In Act III the play has a different setting as follows:

> The wedding band is heard again, quite loud. Lights fade in on the living room. Ed just stares at everyone. Deepali, Ranjit and Bunny react to the raucous tunes and lusty cries of the baraat. Ranjit moves to the windows and shuts it. The music is faint now, except for the occasional whistle or yell. (*CP* 95)

These homosexuals consider marriage between a man and woman unnatural. This is how the conversation goes:

> Ranjit. Why do people get married?
> ...It is so bloody unnatural.
> Ed. What do you mean?
> Ranjit. Oh, we were talking about marriage.
> Bunny. It is natural to the majority of people!
> Ranjit. Animals don't do it. (*CP* 95)

The play moves from drawing room discussion to denouement and the homosexual relationship between Ed and Kamlesh is proved by the photograph found by the watchman. What is worse is that Kamlesh and Sharad's homosexual relationship has also been exposed in the end. The last two movements of the play bring the play to its logical conclusion:

> The guard enters. Sharad looks at the picture of Ed and Kamlesh. He turns the picture away. For the first time the audience notices, the pictures of Ed and Kamlesh in a tight embrace....
>
> Ed (to the guard). Did you...did you take a look at the photograph?
> Guard. Ji...Ji maine kuch nahin dekha....
> Sharad (singing as he goes off stage).
> I ask myself what I have got
> And what I am and what I'm not...
> Exists after a glance at Kamlesh. (*CP* 110-11)

Kiran and Kamlesh hold each other as the play draws to a close. The movements of the play through voice of the articulated characters and the silence of the guiltridden persons show the journey of one's sexual life. Here, normal heterosexual life triumphs over the same-sex love, however real it may be for some people. *Do the Needful* employs the same method of shifting scenes as we find in *Seven Steps Around the Fire.* It begins with "Exterior. Alpesh is in his car driving through a busy street", when Alpesh goes to see Lata for his marriage. The movement of the play is quick from 'Exterior' to 'Interior' (Lata's house). Dattani uses the technique of "Thought" to express the characters's mind. The minds of Lata and Alpesh are known the audience from the beginning of the play. Lata is in love with Salim, a terrorist and Alpesh is a homosexual, who has come to choose Lata as his wife. This is how Dattani presents these two characters:

> Lata (Thought). It is happening, Salim. I do hope you will accept the situation. Will you? I could not careless whether you do or don't, but I will still ask you that when we meet. You would want to make love first, of course. When is just...fine....
>
> Alpesh (Thought). Will you understand me? How much do you really care for me? How much do I really care for you? Do I understand? Is it any easier for you? (*CP* 119-20)

The play moves on from Lata's house to the temple. The parents of both Lata and Alpesh go out to discuss their marriage. The irony is that both Lata and Alpesh think of their own previous affairs. For example, when Alpesh thinks of Trilok, Lata's thought centers round Salim. Thus, she thinks:

> Lata (Thought). Salim, I know you are allowed four wives—what is the point in thinking all that now? I will have to be content keeping you as a lover. How are we going to work this out? What if you have to go back to Kashmir?... I will have to find another lover. I can have more than four.... Why do I think all this? I am a bad girl. I will rot in hell. Oh! Damn the Bangalore Catholic School, sending me on a guilt trip now. (*CP* 127)

With the shift of the location we are shown the "Exterior. The Verandah of the farm house". When Lata knows that Alpesh is a homosexual, she becomes hesitant to marry him, "would it make sense to get married to that lout and make everyone happy?", she asks. With her desire to get her lover Salim, she marries Alpesh, for the latter being a homosexual will have no interest in her. They come to an understanding and get married only to facilitate their own motives of fulfilling love in their own way. Finally, the scene shifts to the road, where the newly wed couple go in a taxi only to go in their own way. Their movement justifies the title of the play, *Do the Needful.*

In *Final Solutions* Dattani introduces an innovative technique of giving two names to a character corresponding to her youth and old age. That character is the mother of Ramnik Gandhi. She is called Daksha in her youth and Hardika after marriage. The movement of the play is shown in the stage directions as follows:

> The stage is dominated by a horseshoe or crescent shaped ramp, with the ends sloping to the stage level. Most of the action of the Mob/Chorus takes place on the ramp. Ideally the Mob/Chorus should remain on stage in a crouched or stylized position throughout the play....
>
> Within the confines of the ramp is a structure suggesting the house of Gandhis with just wooden block for furniture. However, upstage, perhaps on an elevation, is a detailed kitchen and a pooja room.
>
> On another level is a room with a roll top desk and an oil lamp converted to an electric one, suggesting that the period is the late 1940s. This belongs to the young Daksha, who is in fact the grandmother, also sometimes seen as a girl of fifteen. There are several instances when Hardika, the grandmother, and Daksha, the young bride, are on this level at the same time, although they are the same person. (*CP* 166)

The above stage direction shows that the entire play would take place in one place presenting events of history and showing the passage of time as Daksha, a fifteen-year-girl would turn an old grandmother, Hardika. The performance of the play highlights the chorus and the communal violence perpetuated by the mob. "Silence" follows chorus 1, 2 and 3 as a the mob chased the two boys of the other community.

The flashback technique highlights the past of Hardika who married Ramnik Gandhi's father when she was called Daksha. Bobby and Javed took shelter in Ramnik Gandhi's house. In spite of the demand of the Mob, Ramnik refused to hand over them to the mob. Her daughter, Smita supported him but his mother, Hardika and wife, Aruna asked him not to allow these two (Bobby and Javed) to remain in their house. In Act II, the characters remain in the same position as Act I but the interaction among these characters reveals their minds. When Ramnik asked his daughter how she knew them, she hesitantly said that she knew them from her college days (actually she was drawn towards Babban—Bobby during her college career). At this point Hardika asked, "What they were doing in our neighbourhood", to which Bobby replied, "We got lost". In Act III, the spotlight shifts to two men sitting on the floor in a prayer position. "The Muslim chorus is on the highest level of the ramp." Daksha reads from her diary aloud to prove that how the communal feelings have poisoned the minds of the people in our society. The play moves to its logical conclusion with the exit of Bobby and Javed, and Hardika's realization that earlier violence (recorded in her diary) resulted in the looting of shops of one community by another.

It is the stage direction and flashback technique that enhances the performance of the characters. For example, Bobby holds the image of god in Aruna's pooja room and speaks with pride, "look how He rests in my hands!" Then 'the action freezes. Bobby slowly and tenderly replaces the image in the pooja room'. The play reaches its climax with this situation and message of the play becomes implicit. The final solutions of communal tension and violence lie in keeping God above human affairs and false pride.

In *Where There's a Will*, Dattani employs an innovative technique of bringing a deadman, Hasmukh Mehta back to the stage to speak to the audience directly about his feelings for his family. In plays, we know ghosts do appear and speak as in

Elizabethan drama but to make a deadman talk to the audience without the knowledge of other characters, is surely an effective mode of presenting a play as performance. This is how Dattani puts it:

> Hasmukh (to the audience). Have you ever swung on a tamarind tree? Upside down? You should try it some time. You can see the world the way it really is. It's important to get a good grip on the branch with your legs. Then you can relax your hands and head. Like this (*Demonstrates by lying on his back and letting his head and hands dangle over the side of the table.*) How do I look? I don't know about me, but you all definitely look peculiar. (*Points at someone.*) Your shoes need polishing. (*Straightens up.*) That's the way I see my family now. Their lives have been turned upside down since Kiran entered this house. I suppose it was a nasty thing to do. Making Kiran come and live here. You may ask—what kind of a fool would ask his mistress to live with his family? A fool who knows his family very well. Kiran may have been my mistress, but she has far more brains than my wife ever had. But you should see her now, my wife! Transformed. From stupid incapable housewife to clever incapable housewife. Every day is a new lesson for her on husband-understanding. The more time she spends with Kiran, the more she learns about me. The most she learns about me, the more she'll regret having been such a good-for-nothing wife. That will keep her from being a happy widow ever after. One thing I can't stand is a happy widow. There should be a law against them. (*Pause. He resumes his crosslegged position.*) There's one more reason why I sent Kiran here. To keep a check on my daughter-in-law. If there's anyone who has me worried, it's her. She is a clever piece. Might find some loophole in the will. But Kiran is too clever for her. Any woman who is a mistress and a wife has to be clever. (*CP* 496)

In *Thirty Days in September*, the stage is "divided into four acting areas". As stated in Act I all "the action moves without any set changes between scenes". Here Dattani introduces the method of hearing the voice of the characters on tape. Since the play is about incest, this method suits the characters like Mala well. This is equivalent to Hardika reading her diary as Daksha in *Final Solutions*.

In *Clearing the Rubble*, Dattani introduces such devices as 'interior', 'exterior' to show the action inside and outside the house. He has also used the method of 'thought' and 'silence' to bring the past alive before the audience.

Dance Like a Man included in *Collected Plays*, got a new look when Dattani wrote it with Pamela Rooks. So this play co-written with Pamela Rooks and included in *Collected Plays* Vol. II, contains stage innovations. Here we get interior and exterior scenes. The play moves through different places like Dance Hall, Parekh Bungalow, Hallway, Living room, kitchen, bedroom, library street and Shiva temple, courtyard, Dance studio, public garden, open amphi-theatre, garden, bungalow and auditorium. Flashback is the major device by which Dattani makes the character recall their past. The playwright dovetails the surroundings with the mind of the character to make him/her realize the goal in life. After a visit to Shiva Temple, Ratna goes to Chennai Amma's house to learn the art of dancing with perfection. This is how the play moves on:

> Exterior. Shiva temple. Morning. Flashback.
>
> > Idol of Lord Shiva. The aarti is in progress. We pull back to see the poojaris performing the ritual. We move back further to see a crowd of devotees waiting with folded hands for the prasad. Ratna is among them.
> >
> > As the crowds move closer to the shrine, Ratna moves away looking at the people *surreptitiously* to make sure no one notices her. Ratna half runs down the temple steps to a waiting rickshaw. She gets in and the rickshaw driver gets on the cycle and begins to pedal the rickshaw away, just as another rickshaw follows them.
> >
> > Cut to:
>
> Exterior. Street. Morning. Flashback.

> Overheard shot of Ratna in a rickshaw. It comes to a halt in front of a ramshackled building. In fact the whole locality looks quite run-down. On Ratna as she quickly pays the driver and enters the gate to the building.
>
> Exterior. Courtyard. Morning. Flashback.
>
> On Ratna: Having put on her dancing bells she positions herself in front of an ancient crone, Chennai Amma, who sits on a mat on the floor. As Chennai Amma begins to sing a padam beating out the rhythm with a stick, Ratna moves gracefully to the best, interpreting the text on love with facial expressions. Chennai Amma stops to sing. Ratna looks on awaiting some feedback.
>
> Chennai Amma (speaking in an archaic form of Tamil). You won't get the bhava if you do not experience love and devotion. Feel and love and devotion for Shiva. See him as the perfect man. (*CP* II 116-17)

In *Mango Souffle*, *The Swami and Winston*, *Morning Raga*, *Uma and the Fairy Queen* and *Ek Alag Mausam*, Dattani makes use of the same "interior" and "exterior" devices to show the movement of the plays. The interplay of 'silence' and 'sound' adds to the musicality of the plays. His characters move with grace from interior space to outerspace in course of the play. The performance of Dattani's plays depends on the space given to the characters. Needless to say that they strike us as real persons in contemporary society.

Judging by the stage productions, Dattani's plays appeal to us as performing art. The realities of life presented in his plays stare us in our face and we respond to them in empathy. Therein lies Dattani's success as a playwright.

WORKS CITED

Dattani, Mahesh. *Collected Plays*. New Delhi: Penguin Books, India, 2000.

———. *Collected Plays,* Vol II. New Delhi: Penguin Books, India, 2005.

Putting Mahesh Dattani in the Indian English Dramatic Tradition

8

The Indian dramatic tradition dates back to 5th century A.D. when Kalidas published his plays, particularly his *Sakuntala*. Sanskrit literature is the finest of all literary on Indian soil and the repository of Indian literature tradition. The greatest theoretician of dramatic literature is Bharata and his *Natyasastra* (5th c. BC) is the highest achievement in dramaturgy in India. This is older than Aristotle's *Poetics* (330 BC), which is the high watermark in dramaturgy in the west. *Natyasastra* is regarded as the 'Fifth Veda' in India. Having said this, I should hasten to add that I am not concerned with dramatic theory but drama proper—to be precise, the dramatic tradition.

In India, dramas were written in regional literatures (or Bhasha literatures) in imitation of Sanskrit dramas in the long past. Though Indian English drama owes its origin to K.N. Banerjee's *The Persecuted* or *Dramatic Scenes Illustrative of the Present State of Hindu Society in Calcutta* (1831), it is primarily a phenomenon of the twentieth century. In addition to dramas written in the twentieth century, a number of dramas from Bhasha literatures were translated into English. For instance, Vijay Tendulkar, Manoranjan Das, Badal Sircar and a host of others have appeared in English translation. So also Girish Karnad. But Girish Karnad transcreated his plays into English. Hence, he qualifies to be an Indian English dramatist, the sameway as Rabindranath Tagore is called an Indian English poet, dramatist and writer. Nissim Ezekiel has written his *Three Plays* and *Don't Call it Suicide* in English. And Shiv K. Kumar has written a play called, *The Last Wedding Anniversary*. But it is Mahesh Dattani who has given a new direction and sense of purpose to Indian English drama. His two volumes of plays, *Collected Plays* (2000) and *Collected Plays*, Vol. II (2005) are landmarks in Indian English drama. He has won recognition both at home and abroad. B.B.C. has broadcast his plays. The question that baffles us is how to evaluate Dattani's contribution to Indian English drama and how does he portray Indian characters, situations and ethos in his plays.

To make an assessment of Mahesh Dattani as an Indian English dramatist is not an easy task. A multifaceted personality, Dattani has written dramas, radio plays, screen plays and acted in and directed many plays over the years. His plays are primarily written to be staged not to be read as stories in the drawing rooms or classrooms. He is charged by the voice of his characters through the mouth of the actors. That is why, he used to give final shape to some of his plays after they were staged. Drama, unlike poetry or fiction is a performing act. The dialogue of the character and the voice of the actor go together to make a play what it is. Therefore, it is not merely the language of the dialogue but the articulation of it by the actor, which matters in a drama. Dattani's success lies in combining the two artistically in his plays.

Mahesh Dattani, a theatre personality who is actually involved in stage production and performing on the stage, draws inspiration from Marathi playwright Vijay Tendulkar. Unlike Girish Karnad who lays emphasis on history, myths puranas, Dattani concentrates of contemporary society and reality in the fast changing world. I would like to call him a playwright on contemporary urban India and his plays are topical dramas. The questions he addresses in his plays are that of gender, sex, religion, communal tension, feminine identity, same-sex marriage, and above all gay and lesbian relationship. Hence, his plays appear to be both revolting and sometimes, outrageous.

Penguin India has brought out two collections of his plays: *Collected Plays* (2000) and *Collected Plays* (Vol. II) (2005). The first collection contains eight plays such as *Seven Steps Around the Fire*, *On a Muggy Night in Mumbai*, *Do the Needful*, *Final*

Solutions, *Bravely Fought the Queen*, *Tara*, *Dance Like a Man* and *Where There's a Will*. And the second collection contains ten plays—eight new and two of his early plays, *Dance Like a Man* and *Seven Steps Around the Fire*. The eight new plays are *Thirty Days in September*, *Clearing the Rubble*, *Mango Souffle*, *The Swami* and *Winston*, *Morning Raga*, *Uma and the Fairy Queen*, *Ek Alag Mausam* and *The Tale of a Mother Feeding Her Child*. The total corpus of his plays which include Radio plays, Screen plays and Stage plays available in print is sixteen. He came to limelight and sought into fame with the winning of the first ever Sahitya Akademi Award for a playwright in 1998 for his work *Final Solutions* and *Other Plays*.

In his e-mail reply to the present author Dattani stated, 'My earliest influence are non-detailed texts of Shakespeare and BBC recordings of Shakespeare's plays with heavy English accents'. On being asked, 'Does the dramatist's capacity to create memorable characters and events depend on his belief in his theme', Dattani answered, "Absolutely. If the writer does not believe in his theme, how can he expect the audience to believe in anything? But many a time the theme is discovered in the writing. Which means that the theme carried conviction in the writer's awareness of his or her theme, could be a process of discovery".

He also admitted to have been influenced by several Bhasha dramatists such as Vijay Tendulkar, Mahesh Elkunchwar and Madhu Rye. In course of conversation with Utpal K. Banerjee, Dattani states:

> I'm strongly affected by social issues, especially when it comes to power-play in class and gender. A lot of my plays deal with them and they remain the leitmotifs of my plays. I am, however, not a social activist. From my long experience in theatre, I know what will work in a play, that is, what will be empowered writing. My first service is to the story and I believe that the form should serve the content. Usually, there is something like coming to terms at the end and the audience can experience a catharsis-like situation. That's deliberate and is part of my craft! (*Indian Literature* 166)

Dattani brings unusual themes like, hijra marriage, lesbianism, homosexuality, bi-sexuality, dreaded disease like HIV positive into the orbit of Indian English plays. Previously, it was unthinkable to write a play on hijras, but Dattani makes it possible in his well-known play, *Seven Steps Around the Fire*. He dives deep into the psyche of hijras to portray characters like Kamla, Champa and a few other hijras. Added to it is the theme of homosexuality and same-sex marriage. Traditional conformists will run away from the play on the plea that it violets our traditional norms and offends our sensibility. Dattani has the courage of conviction to say what is what. One can't run away from reality, however painful it might be. Dattani not only faces reality but depicts it with all sincerity and devotion.

Dattani's plays such as *Seven Steps Around the Fire*, *Mango Souffle*, *On a Muggy Night in Mumbai*, *Do the Needful* are based on gay and lesbian relationship. Life in these plays are presented from bisexual and same-sex love point of view. By highlighting the problems of hijras in our society, Dattani shows how they are exploited in our society. To treat them as untouchables and again utilizing their services at the time of marriage and childbirth, is to say the least, unfair.

Problems of Indian middle class family such as marriage negotiations, inheritance, poverty caused by natural calamities like earthquakes and droughts are treated as themes in plays like *Where There's a Will*, *Do the Needful*, *Clearing the Rubble*, and *The Tale of a Mother Feeding her Child*. Dattani sees life dwindling under the pressure of poverty and depicts his characters with compassion in his plays. In *Thirty Days in September*, a family play based on incestuous relationship, Dattani shows how women feel humiliated and get exploited by male members of the family. Here, a helpless mother, Shanta turns to Deepak to save her daughter, Mala, for both the mother and the daughter were physically exploited by the same man who happens to be her brother and Mala's uncle. The agonizing request "Please save her. I did not save her. I did not know how to save her. How could I save her when I could not save myself..." (*CP* II 55) rings in our ears over and over again, as we go through the play till the end.

If 'family' and 'gay' themes are central to some of his plays, crime and disease are the focus of three of his plays, *The Swami and Winston*, *Uma and the Fairy Queen*, and *Ek Alag Mausam*. Sitaram Trivedi, a fake religious person wants to cheat people in the name of religion by building Ashrams inside and outside the country. The horror of partition haunts him without end. He tells, Uma, researcher about it emphatically: "What do you know of horrors of partition? I have lived through it!" Dattani exposes the fake sadhus who betray people in the name of religion. Committing crime for sensual gratification is shown in the character of Nila in *Uma and the Fairy Queen*. Nila's killing of Michael, her second husband speaks volumes for her sensual nature and criminal bent of mind. Her son, Feroz calls a spade, a spade:

> She was a famous TV star. Everyone knew her face! She thought she could do whatever she wanted to do. But she was wrong. She was an immoral woman and that something we do not forgive! She slept with her actor friends! For money, for pleasure, or just to please the Devil. And I was born out of her cesspool of lust. (*To Nila.*) You! You don't know what I had to suffer. In school I was known as the bastard! At home I was the unwanted child. We had to move to India and live in hiding to run away from the disgrace, but you won't let us live in peace. Unless you are dead you won't let me live in peace. So die. Prepare to go to hell, mother! (*CP* II 465)

The horror of a dreaded disease HIV positive has shaken the very fabric of the society. Aparna's agonized question to Dr Machado on how to live with George, who is a HIV positive shows our helplessness against that incurable disease. Aparna asks: "How could I carry on with him? How could I when I knew he has HIV positive?" and we are baffled to hear it for we know no answer to it. The only response we can possible give, comes through the mouth of Dr Machado towards the end of the play:

> The Aids virus knows no barriers of caste, creed, religion, age, gender, race. It is not prejudice, fear or ignorance that will win the battle against Aids. But understanding, precaution

and above all love. Today the world over doctors and scientists are trying to find a cure for Aids. In the interest of mankind we hope they succeed. While waiting for that cure to be invested or discovered, let us not forget—that miracles are known to happen. (*CP* II 556-57)

Dattani knows how to close the play which is built on the theme of a fatal disease posing a challenge to the survival of mankind on earth.

Dattani depicts communal distrust and disharmony in his well-known play, *Final Solutions*. The title is highly suggestive, for it makes us think whether the evil of communal violence can be rooted out, lock, stock and barrel. There are hints and guesses in the play which whisper results, provided we pay heed to it. To write a play on a burning topic like this, requires courage of conviction, which Dattani has in plenty. Bobby's reply to Aruna, 'if we understand and believe in one another, nothing can be destroyed", provides a clue to Hindu-Muslim reconciliation and further Bobby adds, "And if you are willing to forget, I am willing to tolerate". This reminds us the great Shakespearean dictum, "forget and forgive". If the Hindus and Muslims forget the past and forgive each other for the wrongs done in the past, then the road to understanding and cooperation will be free of thorns. After all, the past is irrevocable. Why waste the present, for the happenings in the past and destroy our future? This seems to be the message of the play.

Dattani not only deals with the themes like communal violence, crime, homo-eroticism, lesbianism, disease and the breaking down of joint family system, but with finer things of life like dance and music. In *Dancing Like a Man* and *Morning Raga*, he dives deep into the heart of the dancers, artists and singers who pine for recognition. Dance and Music transcend the baser instinct of human beings and bring joy to their minds. It is an irony of life that some people like Amritlal in *Dance Like a Man* and Abhinay's father in *Morning Raga* are opposed to dance and music respectively. But their children remain unfazed and cultivate dance and music against all odds. Dattani suggests through the characters that 'dance' and 'music' can be taken as respectable professions in our society. Old prejudice against dancers and musicians should go. The reviews of Lata's dance speaks volumes for the sublime aspect of dance. It reads like this:

> Her rendition of the ashtapad from *Geeta Govindam* was tenderly intense and intensely tender. The audience was transported to Gokulam and witnessed Radha pining for the divine lover, who has failed to arrive. Lata's tearful expression and heaving bosom conveyed all that was humanly possible. (*CP* II 150)

The love of music and passion for dance are depicted through the characters of protagonists of both the plays. Dattani shows clearly that fulfilment in life comes through the success in music and dance. No doubt, these two plays have added a new dimension to Dattani's plays.

On being asked by the present author (the author met him during the 51st All India English Teachers' Conference at Kolhapur in December 2006), why *Dance Like a Man* ends with Ratna's Voice saying "then we had all the grace, all the brilliance, all the magic to dance like gods?" What do you mean by 'dance like gods?", Dattani answered, "Dance with perfection. In Traditional dance, only Shiv is the perfect dancer".

Dattani's plays could be divided into six broad categories:

(i) Plays on Violence and Crime (*Seven Steps Around the Fire*, *The Swami and Winston*, *Uma and Fairy Queen*, and *Final Solutions*),

(ii) Plays on Gay and Lesbian relationship (*On a Muggy Night in Mumbai*, *Mango Souffle*, *Do the Needful* and here we can also include *Seven Steps Around the Fire*),

(iii) Plays on Natural Calamities (*Clearing the Rubble* and *The Tale of a Mother Feeding Her Child*),

(iv) Family Plays (*Thirty Days in September*, *Bravely Fought the Queen*, *Where There's a Will* and here we can include *Do the Needful*),

(v) Plays on Music and Dance (*Morning Raga* and *Dance Like a Man*),

(vi) Plays on Disease and Disabled (*Ek Alag Mausam* and *Tara*).

Mahesh Dattani always lays emphasis on theatre and the performance of the actor—not on printed words. As Michael Walling puts it:

> To Mahesh, a play is never really finished. Plays only really happen in the theatre, as ephemeral events. The apparently permanent printed text is just one approximation to what might occur when the piece is performed. (*CP* 229)

Having said about Dattani's themes, let me turn to his techniques. Drama as we all know is a performing art. Words in a play assumes significance through articulation by the characters. It is performance on the stage by the actors that influences the audience. Written words don't really matter in a play, as they do in other genres. That is why, the stage direction, movement and setting of the play matter most in our understanding of the texts.

Mahesh Dattani lays emphasis on the articulationary words. All his plays are experimented on the stage and some of his plays were staged first and printed afterwards. As stated earlier a theatre four words matter—they are, movement, stillness, silence, sound, and movement. The setting of the play depends on the arrangement of these four which give it a distinct identity. The movement of the characters and events are governed by stillness, silence and sound.

In order to make his characters life-like on the stage, he too make certain innovations in the techniques of his plays. To make the inner thought in the minds of the characters, he introduced the technique of 'thought' instead of 'asides' in his plays. 'Thought' is followed by 'voice-over' in commensurate with the themes of the play. There is a lot of code-mixing (i.e., Indian words, Hindi words, for example written in English spelling without making an attempt at translation, even when translation is available) in his plays. The language in Dattani's plays transcends gender distinctions. Both men and women use words freely to describe their sex-preferences. The characters are not inhibited. The conflict of the mind cuts across individuals as well as societies. In some of his plays the conflict takes place between characters, and communities and above all, within the same individual. Plays like *Dance Like a Man*, *On a Muggy Night in Mumbai*,

Do the Needful and *Finan Solutions* can be cited as examples here. In this connection I am reminded of Peter Szondi's remarks:

> ...the Drama is primary. It is not a (secondary) representation of something else (primary); it presents itself is itself. Its action like each of its lines, is "original"; it is accomplished as it occurs.... In the Drama, time unfolds as an absolute, linear sequence in the present.... It generates its own time.... This is possible because of the Drama's dialectical structure, which in turn is rooted in interpersonal relationships. (9)

The techniques in Dattani's Plays are in commensurate with his daring portrayal of sex relations and sexual preferences in his plays. If in the past gender, race and class were the determining factors for character analysis, in the nineteen eighties and after sexuality is taken as the most important factor that governs the socio-cultural lives of the people in the metropolis. John McRae's introduction to "on a Muggy Night in Mumbai" underlines this in the following lines:

"Mahesh Dattani is always adventurous in his ways of using the theatrical space at his disposal: multiple levels breaking bounds of the proscenium, wondrously inventive use of lighting to give height, breadth, and depth.... The outside world is always pressing in the heat, the sounds, the people pestering Bunny, the kids who find the photo. Very few dramatists are able to give this sense of a whole society touching the participants in on stage drama it recalls Ibsen at his social best" (*CP* 45).

Dattani's technical virtuosity lies in building tension in a context—Social, Personal or Covertly Political—involving characters and resolving it in the end to the satisfaction of all—Characters as well as audience. Therefore, his plays evoke a sense of empathy among the readers and audience.

The time in Dattani's plays is short. The plays are set in the present and the action takes very limited time—varying from a day to some months. There are flashback techniques as in *Final Solutions* where the old woman goes down the memory lane to recollect her life in her teens. But the play is located in the present. What Peter Szondi speaks in *Theory of the Modern Drama* holds goods for Dattani. He says,

> The dramatist is absent from the Drama. He does not speak; he institutes discussion. The drama is not written, it is set. All the lines spoken in the drama are disclosures. They are spoken in context and remain there. They should in no way be perceived as coming from the author. The drama belongs to the author only as a whole, and this connection is just an incidental aspect of its reality as a work. (8)

Dattani exactly does the same. He raises the issues from sexuality to criminality and then moves on to topical subjects like communal violence, and dreaded disease like Aids and allows the characters to express their views freely. The same technique he adopts with reference to subjects like, music, dance and human relationship. The readers and the audience respond to the dialogues uttered by the characters. His plays evoke a good deal of empathy. His theatrical language modifies his dramatic texts and is reflected in the performance of the characters.

It is true that Dattani has made innovations both in themes and techniques. The question is that what impression his plays leave on the audience. If meaning is made in the plays by interaction and understood in relation to the culture in which they are located, Dattani has little to fear. Like many of the modern plays, in Dattani's works, the similarity between the language of his plays and that of ordinary people in our society is explicit. Each character has his/her distinctive voice. When asked by the present author, "Do you allow your characters or at least the central character to change in course of the play?" Dattani answered, "Yes, very often they have chosen their destiny and I must allow them at times to do what they want to do. But I tend to put them on a train where I am in control of their final destination. What they do during the journey is entirely their business".

Dattani's plays don't idealize the world. They seek to realize it and if possible improve it. That is why, they are neither tragedies nor comedies—they are on contemporary life situations of middle and lower middle class families. The very high (i.e. people at the top politically and economically and the very low (beggars etc.) find no place in his plays. The plays depict real life situations and hence, his characters are life-like, not larger than life. His plays can be best described as Kitchensink dramas based on middle class life. Discrimination against women and female child are clearly portrayed in his plays. He has no gender or communal bias. If in *Tara* discrimination is made against the girl child by her mother, in *The Tale of a Mother Feeding Her Child*, the tenderness of a woman who considers herself as a beloved of the deadman, comes to the fore when she saves the deadman's daughter Shanti risking her life. She took Shanti, to hospital against all odds and saved her life. Dattani has the courage of conviction to expose the people who indulge in corruption, crime and sexual aberration in some of his plays. About the portrayal of sexuality in his plays, it seems, that Dattani has overplayed this theme. Same-sex love may be a reality but it can't be taken as a norm—it is an aberration.

But Dattani has done a commendable job by highlighting the impact of the dreaded disease, Aids in *Ek Alag Mausam*. To write a play on such a theme is to serve the society by making people aware of it. It is timely and urgent. Dattani is right in saying, "The real enemy today is a tiny invisible creature—a virus. The Aids virus knows no barriers of caste, creed, religion, age, gender, race" (*CP* II 556).

Dattani's plays are 'lokadharmi', as opposed to "natyadharmi" of Sanskrit plays. If "natyadharmi" plays conform to the conventions of the theatre, "lokadharmi" caters to the way of the world. In his plays Dattani depicts the characters in contemporary life who reveal themselves before the audience in realistic terms. Some of his plays like *Final Solutions* and *Ek Alag Mausam* which explore social problems raising questions about them and provoke the audience into finding solutions to them could be termed, "Thesis plays". In these plays arguments are manifold but the solutions evade the audience. Dattani examines the problems, find them difficult but does not runaway from them. His characters are lively irrespective of being 'good' and 'evil'. Dattani's characters are 'warm' and human with both virtues and vices. They speak to us in our own situation and evoke a sense of empathy in us. There in lies Dattani's originality.

WORKS CITED

Banerjee, Utpal K. "Utpal K. Banerjee in Conversation with Mahesh Dattani". *Indian Literature.* 48: 5 Sept.-Oct. 2004.

Dattani, Mahesh. *Collected Plays.* New Delhi: Penguin Books, 2000.

———. *Collected Plays*, Vol. II. New Delhi: Penguin Books, 2005.

Szondi, Peter. *Theory of the Modern Drama.* Ed. and Trans. Michael Hays. Cambridge: Polity Press, 1987.

Walling, Michael. "A Note on the Play." *Collected Plays*, New Delhi: Penguin Books, 2000.

Conclusion

9

To make an assessment of Mahesh Dattani as an Indian English dramatist is not an easy task. A multifaceted personality, Dattani has written dramas, radio plays, screen plays and acted in and directed many plays over the years. His plays are primarily written to be staged—not to be read as stories in the drawing rooms or classrooms. He is charmed by the voice of his characters through the mouth of the actors. That is why, he used to give final shape to some of his plays after they were staged. Drama unlike poetry or fiction is a performing act. The dialogue of the character and the voice of the actor go together to make a play what it is. Therefore, it is not merely the language of the dialogue but the articulation of it by the actor, which matters in a drama. Dattani's success likes in combining the two artistically in his plays.

In the concluding chapter of the book, I would like to highlight Mahesh Dattani's contribution to Indian English Drama, in order to place him among other playwrights of our country. Well known theatre personalities like Vijay Tendulkar (Marathi), Badal Sircar (Bengali), Manoranjan Das (Oriya) write in regional languages and are known as Bhasha Playwrights (i.e. playwrights in their respective languages) even when their plays are available in English translation. Girish Karnad is an exception. Though he writes his plays in Kannada, he transcreates them into English and hence, qualifies to be an Indian English playwright. Mahesh Dattani is the only major Indian English playwright writing in English in the closing decades of the twentieth century and now, in the twenty-first century. The question is, wherein does his originality lie? To my mind, his experimentations with new and unusual themes make him what he is today.

Dattani brings unusual themes like hijra marriage, lesbianism, homosexuality, bi-sexuality, dreaded disease like HIV positive into the orbit of Indian English drama. Previously, it was unthinkable to write a play on hijras, but Dattani makes it possible in his well known play, *Seven Steps Around the Fire*. He dives deep into the psyche of hijras to portray characters like Kamla, Champa and a few other hijras. Added to it is the theme of homosexuality and same-sex marriage. Traditional conformists will run away from the play on the plea that it violates our traditional norms and offends our sensibility. Dattani has the courage of conviction to say what is what. One can't run away from reality, however painful it might be. Dattani not only faces reality but depicts it with all sincerity and devotion.

Taboo subjects and words find a place in Dattani's works because he writes topical plays. Take the case of gay and lesbian characters depicted in his plays. Dattani knows that Indian mind does not accept such kind of thing as same-sex love (homosexuality and lesbianism) either in life or in literature. But the fact remains that many people are born like that—they have inclination for same-sex love. And what is more, they want to be united in wed lock as is the case with hetero sexual persons. Dattani has called a spade, a spade. Recently we find well-known writers like Vikram Seth and Shobha De supporting the cause of same-sex marriage.

In course of an interview with Sheela Reddy, the well known Indian English writer, Vikram Seth supports 'gay' and 'lesbian' relationships and pleads for the law to be enacted in this country to legalise same-sex marriage. He says, "it took me long to come to terms with myself. Those were painful years." Here are a few excerpts from the interview:

> When I was young, I came across Section 377 in my mother's law books...
>
> I see myself as Indian, what I don't appreciate is being treated as a criminal in my country.

> We don't give Indian society enough credit. It is not as bigoted as people think....
>
> Historically, we have a tradition of tolerance. We may not talk of things, but we live and let live.
>
> Men think it's unmacho to have feelings for men. But think Caesar, Alexander....
>
> People often concentrate on the sexual...they shy away from thinking of romance, fidelity.
>
> (*Outlook* Oct 2, 2006 52-56)

A number of prominent writers led by Vikram Seth and supported by the Nobel Laureate Amartya Sen protested against Section 377 of the Indian Penal Code. What these writers are pleading for is the freedom of an individual to choose his partner in life, irrespective of sex (i.e. either from same sex or from the opposite sex). This kind of boldness on the part of these writers is an extension of Dattani's opinion on the subject expressed in some of his plays.

There may be no harm in pursuing sexual pleasure in a person of the same sex, but the question of marrying that person creates problems.

Dattani's plays such as *Seven Steps Around the Fire*, *Mango Souffle*, *On a Muggy Night in Mumbai*, *Do the Needful* are based on gay and lesbian relationship. Life in these plays is presented from bisexual and same-sex love point of view. By highlighting the problems of hijras in our society, Dattani shows how they are exploited in our society. To treat them as untouchables and again to utilize their services at the time of marriage and childbirth, speaks volumes for the double standard in our society.

Problems of Indian middle class family such as marriage negotiations, inheritance, poverty caused by natural calamities like earthquakes and droughts are treated as themes in plays like *Where There's a Will*, *Do the Needful*, *Clearing the Rubble*, and *The Tale of a Mother Feeding Her Child*. Dattani sees life dwindling under the pressure of poverty and depicts his characters with compassion in his plays. In *Thirty Days in September*, a family play based on incestuous relationship

Dattani shows how women feel humiliated and get exploited by male members of the family. Here, a helpless mother, Shanta turns to Deepak to save her daughter, Mala for both the mother and the daughter were physically exploited by the same man who happens to be her, brother and Mala's uncle. The agonizing request "please save her. I did not save her. I did not know how to save her. How could I save her when I could not save myself..." (*CP* II 55) rings in our ears over and over again, as we go through the play till the end.

If 'family' and 'gay' themes are central to some of his plays, crime and disease are the focus of three of his plays, *The Swami and Winston*, *Uma and the Fairy Queen*, and *Ek Alag Mausam*. Sitaram Trivedi, a fake religious person wants to cheat people in the name of religion by building Ashrams inside and outside the country. The horror of partition haunts him without end. He tells, Uma, the researcher about it emphatically: "What do you know of horrors of partition? I have lived through it!" Dattani exposes the fake sadhus who betray people in the name of religion. Committing crime for sensual gratification is shown in the character of Nila in *Uma and the Fairy Queen*. Nila's killing of Michael, her second husband speaks volumes for her sensual nature and criminal bent of mind. Her son, Feroz calls a spade, a spade.

"She was a famous TV star. Everyone knew her face! She thought she could do whatever she wanted to do. But she was wrong. She was an immoral woman and that something we do not forgive! She slept with her actor friends! For money, for pleasure, or just to please the Devil. And I was born out of her cesspool of lust. (*To Nila*). You! You don't know what I had to suffer. In school I was known as the bastard! At home I was the unwanted child. We had to move to India and live in hiding to run away from the disgrace, but you won't let us live in peace. Unless you are dead you won't let me live in peace. So die. Prepare to go to hell, mother!" (*CP* II 465).

The horror of a dreaded disease HIV positive has shaken the fabric of the society. Aparna's agonized question to Dr Machado on how to live with George, who is a HIV positive shows our helplessness against that incurable disease. Aparna asks: "How could I carry on with him? How could I when I knew he was HIV positive?" and we are baffled to hear it for we know no answer to it. The only response we can possible give, comes through the mouth of Dr Machado towards the end of the play.

> The Aids virus knows no barriers of caste, creed, religion, age, gender, race. It is not prejudice, fear or ignorance that will win the battle against Aids. But understanding, precaution and above all love. Today the world over, doctors and scientists are trying to find a cure for Aids. In the interest of mankind we hope they succeed. While waiting for that cure to be invested or discovered, let us not forget—that miracles are known to happen. (*CP* II 556-57)

Dattani knows how to close the play which is built on the theme of a fatal disease posing a challenge to the survival of mankind on earth. Dattani depicts communal distrust and disharmony in his well known play *Final Solutions*. The title is highly suggestive, for it makes us think whether there could be an end to religious conflict and resultant communal tension. The distrust between the two communities is so deep-rooted that it defies solutions. Dattani hints at solutions but hesitates to make them plain. It requires courage to admit one's own mistakes. Ramaliklal shows that courage and can be said to represent the authorial voice.

Dattani not only deals with the themes like communal violence, crime, homoeroticism, lesbianism, disease and the breaking down of joint family system, but with finer things of life like dance and music. In *Dance Like a Man* and *Morning Raga*, he dives deep into the heart of the dancers, artists and singers who pine for recognition. Dance and Music transcend the baser instinct of human beings and bring joy to their minds. It is an irony of life that some people, Amritlal in *Dance Like a Man* and Abhinay's father in *Morning Raga* are opposed to dance and music respectively. But their children remain unfazed and cultivate dance and music against all odds. Dattani suggests through the characters that 'dance' and 'music' can be taken as respectable professions in our society. Old prejudice against dancers and musicians should go. The reviews of Lata's dance speaks volumes for the sublime aspect of dance. It reads like this:

> Her rendition of the ashtapad from *Geeta Govindam* was tenderly intense and intensely tender. The audience was transported to Gokulam and witnessed Radha pining for the divine lover, who has failed to arrive. Lata's tearful expression and heaving bosom conveyed all that was humanly possible. (*CP* II 150)

The love of music and passion for dance are depicted through the characters of protagonists in both the plays. Dattani shows clearly that fulfilment in life comes through the success in music and dance. No doubt, these two plays have added a new dimension to Dattani's plays.

Coming to the technical aspect of Dattani's plays, we find there are some intricate problems. For example, two characters—Uma, the research scholar and her husband Suresh, the Superintendent of police appear in three plays—*Seven Steps Around the Fire*, *The Swami and Winston*, and *Uma and the Fairly Queen*. In the introduction to the last mentioned two plays, Jeremy Mortimer writes:

> Another case for the intrepid Uma, daughter-in-law of Bangalore's Deputy Commissioner of Police, and wife of the Superintendent. Still researching her thesis on violence in India and having one solved case to her credit, Uma comes into contact with religious fanaticism at its most extreme when investigating the death of a member of the English aristocracy. (*CP* II 295)

Played out against the backdrop of a hot and bustling Bangalore, a third case, for Uma Rao, intrepid sleuth and wife of Suresh Rao, the Police Superintendent (*CP* II 421).

What is one to make out of these plays, in which the same researcher tries to unveil the truth and bring the culprit to book? Should we take these three plays as a triology on violence and crime? Perhaps, the answer is in the affirmative.

About the portrayal of sexuality in his plays, it seems, that Dattani has overplayed this theme. Same-sex love may be a reality but it can't be taken as a norm—it is an aberration. Since Dattani does not relate his plays to Indian tradition and culture, he seems to plead for gay, lesbian, and bisexual relationships in life. Marriage is consummated on one condition—that is, it must lead to procreation. We are reminded of Eliot's question in *The Waste Land,* "What you get married for if you don't want children?" If the same-sex marriage becomes a law where would procreation come from? Will it not defeat the very purpose of marriage? Dattani has a different answer to this question. That is, all marriages don't lead to procreation.

Dattani's plays don't evoke the myths and legends of ancient India. Here, there is no intertexuality—no going back to the Indian epic or dramatic tradition, as we find in Girish Karnad's plays. (There is only one reference to the *Ramayan* in "Seven Steps Arround the Fire".) His plays are about modern India (Postmodern India, if you like) and contemporary social situations. Like A.K. Ramanujan, Indian English poet, writer and translator, Dattani lays emphasis on family. Family, is the nerve center of his plays. He relates modern Indian families to contemporary reality and re-creates the characters in their situations. Therein lies his appeal to the audience and success as a playwright.

To conclude, I would like to answer two basic questions: (i) What's Dattani contribution to Indian English drama? (ii) In what way he will be a source of inspiration for the dramatists in the twenty-first century? Dattani's contribution lies in bringing every day problems in contemporary society and taboo subjects (i.e., gay and lesbianism) into the realms of drama. Real life situations which stare us in our face are reflected in his plays. His technical innovations in the form of stage directions, 'thought' and 'speech' which represent sub-conscious and conscious mind, conversational idioms, are hallmarks of his plays. Future dramatists will look forward to him for making innovations both in themes and techniques (as he has done in his plays) in their plays. So far as the themes are concerned, only the sky is the limit.

WORKS CITED

Dattani, Mahesh. *Collected Plays.* New Delhi: Penguin Books, 2000.

———. *Collected Plays,* Vol. II. New Delhi: Penguin Books, 2005.

Seth, Vikram. Interview with Sheela Reddy. *Outlook:* 2 October 2006.

Mahesh Dattani in Conversation with Bijay Kumar Das

10

BKD. It is interesting and gratifying for me to have met you during the 51st All India English Teachers' Conference on 27 Dec. 2006. I was deeply moved by your simplicity, humility and insight into human nature. As a playwright you have achieved nationwide fame and earned a name abroad. I would like to begin by asking a simple question. How did you start writing plays?

MD. I began with a need for original writing in English for my amateur theatre group. My formative teen years were spent in trying to establish myself as an actor and director. It was in my mid-twenties, I realized that I wanted to do something closer to my own culture rather than European plays, so it came from a need. I never saw myself as a writer but a theatre person.

BKD. Were you conscious of any kind of dramatic tradition when you started writing?

MD. Unfortunately I was educated in a school where there was little or no stress on Indian literature and drama. So my earliest influences are non-detailed texts of Shakespeare and BBC recordings of Shakespeare's plays with heavy English accents.

BKD. You have written on various themes such as music, dance, disease, human compassion, marriage, same-sex love, gender discrimination, violence, communal tension and above all religious fundamentalism. Which is your favourite theme?

MD. I guess the theme of the triumph of the human spirit over societal oppression seems to be the theme that connects all the issues you mention.

BKD. Do you give more importance to plot or character?

MD. Revealing the human condition through character is my primary focus. The plot is a means to make those revelations stronger and impactful.

BKD. Do you allow your characters or atleast the central character to change in course of the play?

MD. Yes. Very often they have chosen their destiny and I must allow them at times to do what they want to do. But I tend to put them on a train where I am in control of their final destination. What they do during the journey is entirely their business.

BKD. Does the dramatist's capacity to create memorable characters and events depend on his belief in the theme?

MD. Absolutely. If the writer doesn't believe in his theme, how can he expect the audience to believe in anything? But many a times the theme is discovered in the writing. Which means that the theme carried conviction in the writer's subconscious right from the start. The writer's awareness of his or her theme could be a process of discovery.

BKD. In your plays you seem to espouse the cause of the depressed, the downtrodden and the subaltern like hijras, gay and lesbians. Do you want them to be articulate?

MD. I think all these characters are a metaphor for the unspoken and unexpressed within all of us.

BKD. Do you agree with gender critics when they say that homosexuality is as much human as heterosexuality?

MD. Of course, even more so because it goes beyond the animal instinct of sex for procreation.

BKD. You wrote about homosexuality and lesbianism in a number of plays like *Seven Steps Around the Fire*, *On a Muggy Night in Mumbai* and *Do the Needful.* Is homosexualism or lesbianism natural or abnormal?

MD. It is natural although it is not the norm in any of the species. Like being left-handed in a predominantly right handed world.

BKD. Uma, the researcher and her husband Suresh, the Police Officer appear in three plays. What purpose does it serve to keep the same characters in three plays?

MD. Uma Rao is a detective albeit a reluctant one. They are a series.

BKD. Marriage in your plays is a casuality. Do you agree?

MD. Not necessarily although it is hellish. I would say that any relationship is a casuality.

BKD. Do you favour same-sex marriage as the characters in some of your plays desire? If so, what about procreation, which is the main purpose of marriage?

MD. You can be a nurturer and provider in a same-sex marriage just as you can in an opposite sex marriage. Procreation is a choice which some married couples do not exercise. In same-sex marriage procreation is not a choice you have.

BKD. You have brought out the significance of dance and music in two of your plays. *Dance like a Man* ends with Ratna's voice saying "then we had all the grace, all the brilliance, all the magic to dance like gods"? What do you mean by "dance like gods"?

MD. Dance with perfection. In traditional dance, only Shiva is the perfect dancer.

BKD. *Thirty Days in September* deals with the theme of incest. Did Shanta forgive Mala in the end of the play?

MD. Her closing line to Mala is 'it was not your fault, so there is nothing to forgive'. I think when both Mala and Shanta realize that it wasn't each others fault there is a true resolution to their conflict.

BKD. Why did you retain the title of your play *Ek Alag Mausam* without translating into English? Can we take the play as a didactic one?

MD. It is a screenplay and not a stage play. It was a commissioned piece with a definite message of Aids awareness. I did translate the title to "A Special Season" but somehow everyone preferred my original title.

BKD. *Final Solutions* is a play on communal hatred and disharmony. If some people of one community find fault with the superstitions in their religion, why can't the people of another community see the negative aspect of their religion?

MD. It takes a great deal of confidence and courage to be self-critical. Being blind to one's failings is a weakness and not a matter of pride. If we as Hindus can criticize ourselves that should be seen as a virtue rather than a failing. Sweeping things under the carpet does not make a society grow or remain functional.

BKD. Why should a character get two names like Daksha and Hardika in the same play?

MD. Where I come from in traditional families, a woman has to change her name to suit the rashi of her husband, I have used it as a metaphor for what Daksha has to give up to conform to her new home. This migration from babul to piya ka ghar is also a metaphor for the cross migration that took place.

BKD. Do you have a message to be conveyed to the people and the society through your plays?

MD. I am not sure whether I have a message. If my plays make an audience reflect on the characters and their motives, either critically or in appreciation I would feel fulfilled.

BKD. Your plays have elaborate stage directions. You have used two modes—'thought' and 'voice-over' in your plays. Why do you put it like this?

MD. In radio drama, thoughts are processed differently in recordings, so the need to differentiate between what is a 'voice-over' or sutradhar or inner thought.

BKD. How can a deadman exchange words with the living as you have done in the character of Hasmukh?

MD. In theatre, reconfiguring time, space and movement is where the art is.

BKD. Why didn't you recreate history, myths, folktales and legends in your plays?

MD. I am not sure how convincing I would be. Besides I have my own stories to tell based on life around me as I see it.

BKD. How do you organize Space, Time and Movement in your plays?

MD. I use parallel action in series time sometimes or use memory as a selling to move in time.

BKD. My last question. Could you tell us something about what you are involved in writing now?

MD. I have just completed a radio play 'The Girl Who Touched the Stars' for BBC Radio.

Bibliography

Primary Sources

Dattani Mahesh, *Collected Plays*. New Delhi: Penguin Publishers, 2000.

———. *Collected Plays*, Vol. II. New Delhi: Penguin Publishers, 2005.

Secondary Sources

Avens, Sally. "A Note on the Play", *Do the Needful. Collected Plays*. New Delhi: Penguin Books, 2000.

Azmi, Shabana. "A Note on the Play", *Morning Raga. Collected Plays,* Vol. II. New Delhi: Penguin Books, 2005.

Babu, M. Sarat. *Indian Drama Today*. New Delhi: Prestige, 1977.

Bhatta, S. Krishna. *'Indian English Drama': A Critical Study*. New Delhi: Sterling, 1987.

Chaudhuri, Asha Kuthari, *Mahesh Dattani: An Introduction*. New Delhi: Foundation, 2005.

Das, Bijay Kumar, *Postmodern Indian English Literature*. New Delhi: Atlantic Publishers and Distributors (P) Ltd., 2003.

Dalmia, Vasudha: *Poetics, Plays and Performances: The Politics of Modern Indian Theatre*. New Delhi: OUP, 2006.

Dattani, Mahesh, "Contemporary Indian Theatre and its Relevance" in *Journal of Indian Writing in English*, 30:1 (Jan. 2002).

Devanesen, Mithran. "A Note on the Play". *Dance Like a Man. Collected Plays.* New Delhi: Penguin Books, 2000.

Dhawan, R.K. and Tanu Pant, ed. *The Plays of Mahesh Dattani: A Critical Response.* New Delhi, Prestige, 2005.

Dubey, Lillete. "A Note on the Play". *Thirty Days in September. Collected Plays,* Vol. II. New Delhi: Penguin Books, 2005.

Iyengar, K.R.S. *Indian Writing in English.* Bombay: Asia Publishing House, 1962.

Kakar, Sudhir. The Inner World: *A Psychoanalytic Study of Childhood and Society in India.* New Delhi: Oxford University Press, 1991.

Kushwaha, M.S., ed. *Dramatic Theory and Practice: Indian and Western.* New Delhi: Creative Books, 2000.

McRae, John. 'A Note on the Play'. *On a Muggy Night in Mumbai. Collected Plays.* New Delhi: Penguin Books, 2000.

Mee, Erin. "A Note on the Play". *Tara. Collected Plays.* New Delhi: Penguin Books, 2006.

Mortimer, Jeremy. "A Note on the Play". *Seven Steps Around the Fire. Collected Plays.* New Delhi: Penguin Books, 2000.

———. "Introduction". *Collected Plays* Vol. II. New Delhi: Penguin Books, 2005.

———. "A Note on the Play". *Clearing the Rubble. Collected Plays,* Vol. II. New Delhi: Penguin Books, 2005.

———. "A Note on the Play". *The Swami and Winston. Collected plays,* Vol. II. New Delhi: Penguin Books, 2005.

———. "A Note on the Play". *Uma and the Fairy Queen. Collected Plays,* Vol. II. New Delhi: Penguin Books, 2005.

———. "A Note on the Play". *The Tale of a Mother Feeding Her Child. Collected Plays,* Vol. II. New Delhi: Penguin Books, 2005.

Multani, Anglie, ed. *Mahesh Dattani's Plays: Critical Perspectives.* New Delhi: Pencraft International, 2007.

Myles, Anita. "The Subaltern Woman: A Critique'. *The Spiel Journal of English Studies,* 1:2 (July 2005).

Naik, M.K. and Shyamala A. Narayan *Indian English Literature, 1980-2000: A Critical Study*. New Delhi: Pencraft International, 2001.

Narasimhaiah, C.D., ed. *Makers of Indian English Literature*. New Delhi: Pencraft International, 2000.

Padamsee, Alyque. "A Note on the Play". *Final Solutions. Collected Plays*. New Delhi: Penguin Books, 2000.

Pandey, Sudhakar and Freya Barua, ed. *New Directions in Indian Drama*. New Delhi: Prestige, 1994.

Pickering, Kenneth. *How to Study Modern Drama*. London: The Macmillan Press Ltd., 1988.

Raina, Sita. "A Note on the Play". *Where There's a Will. Collected Plays*. New Delhi: Penguin Books, 2000.

Rao, Kshama. *'Mahesh Dattani'*, The Gentleman. (March 2003).

Reddy, K. Venkata and Dhawan, R.K., ed. *Flowering of Indian Drama*. New Delhi: Prestige, 2004.

Rice, Philip and Patricia Waugh, ed. *Modern Literary Theory*. London: Arnold, 2002.

Sen, Sudeep. *'Mahesh Dattani's Play Opens in England'*. 'The Gentleman', June 1996.

Shah, Sanjeev. "A Note on the Screen Play". *Mango Souffle*. New Delhi: Penguin Books, 2005.

Subramanyam, Laxmi, ed. *Muffled Voices: Women in Modern Indian Theatre*. New Delhi: Shakti, 2002.

Szondi, Peter. *Theory of Modern Drama*. Trans. and Ed. Michael Hays. Cambridge: Polity Press, 1987.

Index